I've had the privilege of know
friend, customer, and physicia
rooms in our house. She has
countless people. Her enthusiasm for life can't be denied. Her extraordinary
life and commitment are inspiring. Her readers who make the trip to Valley
Head, Alabama, to get their books signed will be in for the treat of their lives!

—Mark Thel, MD FACC

Valinda Miracle can only be described as her last name implies—a modern-day miracle. Her testimony is one that would be comparable to those read about in the Gospels of Matthew, Mark, Luke, and John. Valinda's book, *The Dead Don't Bleed*, describes in detail how faith in the living God, the Creator of the body, can sustain the whole body physically, emotionally, mentally, and, most importantly, spiritually. This book will help you know the love of God in a supernatural way. It will help you overcome the fears and disappointments in life. Valinda knows the agony of defeat, but when Jesus came on the scene, she experienced the joy of success. Very few people will impact your life like you will be impacted as you read about this woman's life and her faith in God. As a friend and sister in the Lord, I thank God that He has allowed Valinda Miracle to be a part of my life. As you read her book, I believe you will feel as I do.

—Elaine Hollmer, International Evangelist
Elaine Hollmer Ministries

Ezk 16:6

THE
DEAD
DON'T
BLEED

THE DEAD DON'T BLEED

THOSE WHO ARE ALIVE DO

VALINDA MIRACLE

CREATION HOUSE

THE DEAD DON'T BLEED by Valinda Miracle
Published by Creation House
A Charisma Media Company
600 Rinehart Road
Lake Mary, Florida 32746
www.charismamedia.com

Unless otherwise noted, all Scripture quotations are from the Holy Bible, New International Version of the Bible. Copyright © 1973, 1978, 1984, International Bible Society. Used by permission.

Scripture quotations marked KJV are from the King James Version of the Bible.

Scripture quotations marked AMP are from the Amplified Bible. Old Testament copyright © 1965, 1987 by the Zondervan Corporation. The Amplified New Testament copyright © 1954, 1958, 1987 by the Lockman Foundation. Used by permission.

Scripture quotations marked NKJV are from the New King James Version of the Bible. Copyright © 1979, 1980, 1982 by Thomas Nelson, Inc., publishers. Used by permission.

Scripture quotations marked The Message are from The Message: The Bible in Contemporary English, copyright © 1993, 1994, 1995, 1996, 2000, 2001, 2002. Used by permission of NavPress Publishing Group.

Design Director: Bill Johnson
Cover design by Terry Clifton

Visit the author's Web site: miraclepottery.com

Library of Congress Cataloging-in-Publication Data: 2012940593
International Standard Book Number: 978-1-62136-070-4 (hardback)
International Standard Book Number: 978-1-61638-939-0 (softback)
E-book International Standard Book Number: 978-1-61638-940-6

While the author has made every effort to provide accurate telephone numbers and Internet addresses at the time of publication, neither the publisher nor the author assumes any responsibility for errors or for changes that occur after publication.

First edition

12 13 14 15 16 — 9 8 7 6 5 4 3 2 1
Printed in Canada

ACKNOWLEDGEMENTS

To Phil and Spence:

Thank you for letting me grow up *with* you, for allowing me to experience *with* you the childhood I never had. And for all your love and effort in encouraging, supporting, and understanding me through each phase of our lives together. I will forever be grateful. *I am so very proud of both of you!*

To Bill and Barbara:

Thank you—*and Phil and Spence, as well*—for being there for me through all the illnesses and challenges of other sorts, for continuously undergirding me in prayer and in so many additional ways day after day and night after night. And thank you, therefore, for all the wonderful, beautiful times of fun and celebration you helped my heavenly Father make possible—as He, so amazingly gracious and merciful, has been faithful to do exceedingly, abundantly above what I could have ever asked or thought. *I love you all!*

"Oh, look. It's bleeding! *Dead skin doesn't bleed!*"
That's what the doctor said when the bandages were
    removed.
This meant that Valinda Miracle would live,
that the flesh-eating disease had not won.
Divorce, drowning, and death;
abortion, accidents, and abandonment;
robbery and rape—these did not win either.

A TRUE STORY

CONTENTS

FOREWORD

IT'S A MIRACLE STORY

THIS BOOK'S AUTHOR is a marketplace success in the pottery-making business. Her cozy and captivating Miracle Pottery & Art Gallery, tucked on a hillside in Mentone, Alabama, is called Miracle Pottery and *not* for the mere reason that Miracle is Valinda's last name.

Her answer to the oft-asked question as to how she came to be so accomplished in the ceramic arts is, "It's a *miracle* that I *can* make pottery." Then she goes on to explain that, first, she doesn't have any extensive or professional training in this craft. And second, she at one time had a tremendous handicap that absolutely disqualified her from ever doing what she is today.

For all practical purposes, a *number* of traumatic, even near-death experiences positioned this woman for anything but the success story that is hers. But then she has as well been blessed with one miraculous rescue and recovery after another; and she attributes them *all* to God, with none comparing to her miraculous experience of *the love of Jesus Christ*—so wondrous, inexplicable, and unfathomable; unearned, unmerited, and free. Valinda so strongly testifies to this *miracle of miracles in her life* that Jesus Himself, not this woman, becomes the leading character in her story.

NOT A POT ABOUT POTS

One way of classifying ceramic art is according to its overall purpose. It is either a functional creation intended to be used or one that commemorates a tradition, as in a craft that is intended to be passed down from generation to generation without actually having participated in it. The latter is said to be "pots about pots." These pots might have all the right parts—as in a lid, a handle, and a spout—but like I said, they are not intended to be used.[1]

They sit on the shelf, even behind glass doors, looking pretty, but have never held hot gravy or cold potato salad, been passed around at a dinner table or dunked in dishwater or towel-dried with human hands—having risked being chipped, cracked, even broken, and having to have their pieces glued back into place if not altogether trashed.

Keeping this in mind, there is an abundance of voices in the land today. But how credible are these voices? Do they *know about* something, or do they actually *know* that something, having *personal* knowledge of it? In other words, are they pots that have been involved in some way or other with what they are sharing, or are they merely "pots *about* pots"?

With this said, Valinda is not a "pot *about* pots." She has been fashioned on the potter's wheel of *life* and fired and fortified in *life's* kiln and has come out to be a credible voice to those who need understanding and help in, well, *in what?*

Well, let's see. Apostle Paul was chosen to write around two-thirds of the New Testament, and he said of himself:

> Five times I received from the Jews the forty lashes minus one. Three times I was beaten with rods, once I was stoned, three times I was shipwrecked, I spent a night and a day in the open sea, I have been constantly on the move. I have been in danger from rivers...bandits...my own countrymen...from Gentiles...in the city...in the country...at sea...from false brothers. I have labored and toiled...often gone without sleep...known hunger and thirst...often gone without food...cold and naked.
> —2 Corinthians 11:24–27

What kind of labors and flogging and prisons and deaths can this book's author bring to bear that might make her someone who can feel our pain and be able to tell us how to work *through* it? Because she did just that—she worked *through* her pain in all its ramifications! This is what some of her experiences have looked like:

> Left motherless and to take care of a three-year-old sister *and* a father at age nine; abused as a child; betrayed in marriage and divorced; held down four jobs at a time; was raped; went through an abortion; survived suicide attempts, vehicle accidents, drowning, and electrical shock; flat-lined four times; suffered a closed head injury; was put at death's door by a negligent doctor; was attacked by the flesh-eating disease; endured open-heart surgery; *and* has gone without sleep and food and had to deal with a bandit or two and even some heat stroke, scorpions, and tarantulas on the mission field.

Yes, this is *all* true. Every bit of it! And I know—it has the appearance of the mafia from hell having put out a contract on this individual since she was a child. And maybe so!

I also am well aware of the great concern that might be expressed by oh so very many at this point: *Where are this woman's credentials when it comes to having faith and enjoying divine protection as a Christian? Why wasn't the enemy kept at bay in all these times of tragedy and trial?* And I ask you, "Where were Paul's credentials in these areas when he went through all he did?"

In the New Testament, we find God miraculously delivering Paul and Silas from prison with an earthquake (Acts 16:25–26). You don't get stories of being miraculously delivered from prison without someone having been in prison. We read of Paul and an entire crew being miraculously delivered from a shipwreck at sea (Acts 27). You don't get stories of being miraculously delivered from a shipwreck at sea without someone having been in a shipwreck. We read of Paul being miraculously spared when a venomous snake bit him (Acts 28:3–5). You don't get stories of being miraculously delivered from the bite of a venomous snake without someone having been bit. And it's interesting that those looking on initially thought Paul to be "some bad case," as in a murderer, just because the snake had fastened itself to his hand; but when he didn't drop dead, they changed their mind and said he was a god (Acts 28:4–6). *Interesting.*

There is definitely a difference between *hearing about truth* and *hearing from someone who has experienced that truth*. Valinda's experiences have certainly given her some credentials when it comes to certain matters, including believability and authority, and have certainly positioned her to be able to comfort you with the comfort wherewith she has been comforted.

Her story in essence offers a one-stop shopping spree for what it takes to see your mess turned into a masterpiece, for working with God to see what the enemy meant for evil turned around for your good, and most importantly, for getting to know God on a level that perhaps you never knew Him before. You will certainly have a greater revelation of His love when you reach this book's end, and you *will* walk away to *live loved* by Him. And if you don't know what that means—to *live loved*—then you really need to read this story.

And there is more. This book is not all about coming through your messes victorious. *The Dead Don't Bleed* doesn't just offer you wisdom to get through your storms but wisdom to not get into some of them in the first place.

THE DEAD DON'T BLEED. ALIVE PEOPLE DO!

Know assuredly that this book's author, just like Paul, does *not* glorify sickness, disease, or calamity, nor calls them the handiwork of God. It's just that troubles and persecutions are real. Catastrophes happen. This book does not deal with all the whys in regard to why bad things happen to good people, but it does produce some understanding as to how God works in the midst of these bad things and how we can embrace Him in our worst times to truly see our messes turned around.

Don't think for one minute that this volume's journey is about Valinda's tragedies—about being drowned, driven over, divorced, and diseased; about enduring an abortion, accidents, abandonment, robbery, and rape. Granted, healings call for something that needs to be healed. Miracles call for impossible situations. Resurrection power can't be experienced without something being dead. But the *focus* of this story is on the *healings*, *miracles*, and *resurrection power*—not on sickness and disease, impossible situations, and death. Because dead skin doesn't bleed, then the bleeding meant that the individual at risk *was alive*. The flesh-eating disease *did not win*. That's the *real* story!

—BOBBIE JO HAMILTON,
I AM MINISTRIES

PART I

PATHS NOT CHOSEN

Chapter 1

UNLOVED, UNWANTED, AND ALONE

NOT EVERYONE HAS the option of choosing his or her path. Not everyone's negative past—or at least parts of it—is the result of poor judgment, wrong decisions, selfish living, and the like. At age nine, I found my young, twenty-seven-year-old mother dead. I had returned from school to be met by my three-year-old sister, who told me that our mother was "awfully sick." As it turned out, our mother had been dead about six hours. The cause of her death was never really determined.

On that horribly fateful day, I felt my world had abruptly ended, but the truth of the matter was that only my world as a happy little girl had come to an end. A world of being unloved and unwanted, a world of mean and cruel abuse was about to begin.

I had excitedly run all through the house that afternoon after school calling for my mother because I had made a good grade on a test that I had been worried about, and I was eager, as well, to tell my mom how the kids had liked the new dress that she had made for me just the day before.

Finally checking the outside toilet and finding my mother's lifeless body, already swollen, black, and blue, I desperately ran for help, praying the entire way to the neighbor's house, "Please, dear God, let my mommy be alright." But, even at nine, I had already become acquainted with the appearance and feel of death. I knew somehow in my heart that my mother was even then in heaven—along with everyone and everything else that I had ever loved.

EVERYTHING THAT I LOVED DIED

I remembered standing by the side of my precious grandmother holding her hand when she died when I was about five years old. And then there was my favorite uncle, my mom's brother. While serving in Korea he would send me special things, like dolls. I had hardly been able to wait for him to return home from the armed services, and when he did, we were big buds. He was a tall, heavy-built man who would carry me around on his shoulders, and sometimes after fashioning a swing for me with his hands he would bend over and sway me back and forth. He kept me with him practically everywhere he went; I absolutely loved him. But then, after managing to survive all the possible horrors and tragedies of Korea, he was killed in an automobile accident.

On top of that, every pet I had ever owned, with the exception of Mutt, met with some untimely death. Mutt was my Cocker Spaniel. Somehow knowing that I loved animals, she would very gingerly latch on to baby rabbits and squirrels and bring them to me still very much alive. I ended up with a cemetery full of pets as they died one after the other.

When my uncle died, *all* my love was turned to Mom. She would stay up throughout the night trying to save one of my little pets but seemingly always to no avail. She would once again gather me in her arms to assure me that everything would be alright as my little animal friend was now in heaven and in God's hands. Then she would help me make a pretty box to bury my pet in.

I absolutely loved my mother, and we were always working together. We picked berries together. We canned together. We took care of the garden together. Depending on what time we would be working in the garden, she would have most of the evening meal already cooking, and she would at one point look up at me and say, "Honey, it's getting about time for your daddy to come home. Run in the house and put on a pan of cornbread."

At that time I was only seven or eight years old, but I'd run into the house, prepare the cornbread, and put it in the oven. The day before I found my mom dead, we had shelled a whole big tub of peas. *Together.*

Three and one-half months pregnant she was at that time. Her autopsy stated the cause of death to be "pneumonia fever." But those in charge said they just put that down because they didn't really know what killed her; they never really knew.

So my grandmother, my uncle, and then my mom—within a short, three-year period, they all died. And all those little animals had died. Almost everything that I ever loved had died, and somehow I came to blame myself, that I was causing them to die. I concluded that in loving them I had caused them to die.

Consequently, I became bitter for many, many years. I would not allow myself to love—because I was afraid if I loved anybody or any little animal, I would cause him or her to die. And I went through a good portion of my young life feeling that way. It took me years to be able to truly love again.

HOME . . . ALONE

My mother didn't realize she was voicing a prophecy when she came home from the hospital with my tiny baby sister, Barbara. I was six years old, and Mother very carefully laid Barbara in my lap and said, "I brought you a little baby home for you to take care of. *She's yours.*"

I thought, "Oh, this is so wonderful," because I loved dolls. All of a sudden I had a real, live baby doll. And, boy, did I spend all of my time that I could running to get her bottles and running to get her diapers, and I'd even wash out her diapers for her. You know, back then you didn't have disposable diapers like Pampers and Huggies; you had cloth ones. And it wasn't a chore for me at all to wash out my sister's diapers, because I loved her so much.

I was so glad to help Mama all I could in taking care of that baby girl. She was the sweetest and prettiest little thing. But Mother didn't realize what she was saying when she told me, "I brought you a little baby home for you to take care of. *She's yours*"—because close to two and one-half years later, Mother died. And then it was my responsibility to take care of that baby girl.

I had been left at home alone to take care of not only myself but a toddler—and then my father as well. My mother was known for growing all our food, canning it for the winter, making all our clothes and quilts, taking care of the home repairs, even the lawn; yet she still found time for cooking, cleaning, doing the laundry, in addition to helping needy family members, neighbors, and friends. I had enjoyed helping my mother with all these tasks, but now, for the most part, they all had come to rest on my young shoulders.

I had virtually no understanding or help from my father. I would get up at 4:30 each morning, cook bacon and eggs, gravy, and biscuits—homemade biscuits because my father did not like the canned ones or toast. It was a struggle to get all our clothes together for Dad to go to work and me to go to school and my sister, Barbara, to be ready for the babysitter and, in later years, to go to school. But somehow by the grace of God I managed day after day.

There was never a kind word from my father, only criticism and even more demands. He seemed to somehow blame me for the tragedy of my mother's death when he was twenty-nine, of losing his wife and having his world come tumbling down. He was left to raise a near-three-year-old and a nine-year-old—something he knew nothing about. His wife had always taken care of everything, even laying out his clothes and putting his food on his plate. What was he to do now?

I don't remember alcohol being a major problem in my dad's life up to that time, but after my mother's death the way he managed to deal with life was unfortunately at the bottom of a bottle, turning to alcohol and drinking buddies for the comfort he needed. His giving little to no thought about money or food or necessities for the home resulted in even more frustration and stronger demands being placed on my shoulders. There was more cursing and name-calling when I simply could not do all that Mother had managed to do for our family and home. Needing my dad's love and approval now more than ever, I worked all the harder to please him.

Chapter 2

ABUSE AND DYSFUNCTIONAL THEOLOGY

M Y DAD HAD come from a long line of alcoholics. And now, along with his drinking buddies, there were his dad and brother who came on the scene. And they in their drunkenness tore at my clothes, bringing on more abuse. I learned to fight like a tiger and hide in the woods till they were all gone. I was afraid to tell anyone what was happening, because not only was I blaming myself for all the deaths in my life, but I thought this abusive treatment was somehow my fault as well.

Whether consciously or subconsciously I wrestled with all kinds of tormenting thoughts: "I can't do things right; I can't ever do enough." "If I could, then my dad wouldn't be so disappointed and upset with me." "I'm not smart enough or pretty enough." "There is some reason why my dad doesn't love me as much as he loves my sister." "There are just things about me that make people not want to love and treat me right." And then there were those feelings that come with being abused—feelings of being soiled, damaged, worthless, and even ashamed.

Even when a young girl, I knew there was a great big God out there somewhere. But when I prayed, I thought, "He won't hear and answer my prayers. How could God love me if no one else does? How could He love someone who causes people to die and causes people to abuse her? Why would God want anything to do with me, because I am a good-for-nothing?"

For those whose past does not involve abuse—whether mental, physical, sexual, or otherwise—it can come across perplexing that a person who has endured this harmful, offensive treatment would somehow consider herself (or himself) personally responsible, as having caused or deserved this mistreatment. But sadly, often the victim simply does not have the equipment—the understanding or the mental, emotional, social, even spiritual maturity—to see this kind of *situation for what it really is*. In his book *Messy Spirituality*, Michael Yaconelli writes, "Too many carry the scars of physical, mental, or psychological abuse, awakening each day to the haunting memories of a time when they were acted upon, against their will, and now find themselves hopelessly trapped between facing their past or running from it."[1]

Now, I don't pretend to be an authority when it comes to every ramification of this subject, and I do not intend to put forth some deep and thorough theological discussion in this regard; but I have some thoughts I want to share, because this is one of those places that I've been—both as a child and as a wife. I believe I have some thoughts to share that a great many (especially those who have been abused) have thought but have not voiced. Maybe I can be a voice for someone—maybe a lot of someones—that will clear up their misconceptions of God and how He deals with His created beings, even setting them free from guilt and torment that has been imposed on them by their own ignorance or even that of a church that has sorely misrepresented our Lord.

I don't just believe there has been some tragic mishandling of abusive situations in Christian ranks, especially in marriages. I *know* this has been then case. Not understanding our God (who He *really* is) and His relationship with us, who are *His* created beings, has resulted in a dysfunctional theological belief system that has handed out some dreadful rulings to people caught in these threatening places.

Great minds—great men and women of God—have had to look at Scriptures more closely in regard to abuse of all kinds and rethink them in the light of "precept upon precept; line upon line" (Isa. 28:10, kjv). They have had to examine them in the light of the promise that "He has made us competent ministers of a new covenant—*not of the letter but of the Spirit; for the letter kills, but the Spirit gives life*" (2 Cor. 3:6, emphasis added) and in the light of the mandate that the Word and the Spirit must be in agreement. (See 1 John 5:8.) Mind you, the Word of God doesn't' change; but our understanding of it has. Our revelation of it has grown.

What Jesus tells us in Mark 12:30–31 involves the *whole* aspect of being human: "Love the Lord your God with all your *heart* and with all your *soul* and with all your *mind* and with all your *strength*. The second [commandment] is this: 'Love your neighbor as yourself'" (emphasis added). And the same is true in 3 John 2: "Dear friend, I pray that you may enjoy good health and that *all* may go well with you, even as your soul is getting along well" (emphasis added). Jesus is interested in the whole person and connects love with action. His theology calls for what Maxine O'Dell Gernert refers to as "a tight, bonded responsibility between devotional belief and behavioral reality."[2] Neither Jesus, the living Word, nor His Holy Spirit is ever responsible or supportive of behavior that is inconsistent with what the Word tells us is right.

The "letter" only of the Word, without the agreement of the Spirit, has been used to kill—even *literally*—innocent souls. Mean, harmful, and wrong things have been done in the name of God—claiming to be God's doings when they weren't, claiming to be God's doings when He had absolutely nothing to do with them. They were sometimes done while claiming to be abiding by the scriptural principles of headship, submission, and authority.

I stated that often the abuse victim simply does not have the equipment—the understanding and maturity—to see the abusive situation for what it is. There have been those who knew something was terribly wrong, but they felt powerless to escape the environment where the abuse, often repeatedly, took place. That is quite understandable when it comes to a child. I know. I know that feeling of powerlessness that a child can have. But then there are adults who remain in an abusive situation because their stunted understanding of Scripture tells them it is their Christian responsibility to remain with their abuser and that to do otherwise would be to go against the will of God. I know that feeling as well. Rationale for staying in an abusive situation too many times has been affirmed, even handed out, by the church—yes, by those in leadership or authority who the victim actually sought out for help.

Like I said, this is not meant to be some treatise on abuse; but, in failing to address this subject, I would have robbed my story of some of its power by missing the opportunity to help someone else in an area where my suffering has been great, even torturous. And had it not been for the goodness and mercy of God, my situation would have been *deadly*.

The bottom line is, according to Walter Brueggemann: abuse is "a violation of the innate, sacred right to life and safety...a transgression against another's personhood...taking that which belongs to another...robbing value from another life."[3] As Gernert explains, with human beings having been created in the image of God, abuse, at its heart, is an irreverent crime against "the holiness of the creation and the essence of God"[4] in that creation. It is misused power, "behavior that manipulates relationship in order to meet the needs for self-gratification."[5] It is the opposite of the Jesus-kind of power; it aims at controlling people, whom God Himself does not aim to control but rather gives the freedom to choose to love and obey Him. It might come as a surprise to a great many that God is not interested in controlling human beings. He said that His people "will offer themselves willingly" (Ps. 110:3, AMP). Our Father is interested in people choosing to love and obey Him, not in them being coerced to do so.

Just like the God of the Bible speaks of *giving to receive* and *dying to live*, His idea of power is that "whosoever will be great among you, let him be your minister," and "whosoever will be chief among you, let him be your servant" (Matt. 20:26–27, KJV). He reveals power as "self-emptying," portrayed by a basin and towel as opposed to "clinched fists and clubs."[6]

And clinched fists and clubs come in different shapes and sizes and forms. Words can be clinched fists and clubs. They, according to Scripture, can be "forceful" (Job 6:25, NKJV), "drawn swords" (Ps. 55:21), "arrows" (Ps. 64:3), "wounds" (Prov. 18:8, KJV), and "death" (Prov. 18:21). Physical abuse is only one of the hats this improper use of power wears. There are such things as mental, emotional, and spiritual blows that can be so severe as to take away individuals' control of their life, to put them in a place of helplessness where they can no longer go on—where they no longer have strength to help themselves, where their very survival is at stake. We are not just physical beings. We can be walking around very much physically alive but mentally incapacitated and emotionally dead. I point this out because when we think of abusive situations we tend to think only of those that leave physical scars.

Keeping in mind that I am well aware of the spiritual principle of being quick to forgive offenses and go on with our lives, let's consider, for example, a mate (let's say the husband) that continues doing something mentally abusive (violating his partner's sacred right to dignity and life) day after day after day after day; and that partner forgives him day after day after day after day, even month after month and year after year. Because it's not physical abuse, the effects of which are worn on the outside of the body, outsiders may find it difficult to understand why the abused mate reaches a place of screaming that she has had enough, that she can't take it anymore, that she's got to get out of the situation because it is destroying her.

She has forgiven and forgiven and forgiven and gone on living and living and living. Her mate is not physically beating her up, but he is viciously and often, even continually, attacking her mentally—dealing the kind of blows that are so severe as to take away her control of her life, to put her in a place of helplessness where her very existence is at stake.

Because people can't *see* her mental or emotional wounds, they don't understand where she's at. You can *see* physical scars, but you can't see mental and emotional ones. But the latter kinds of wounds can be just as deep, if not deeper, and just as bad. And they have their way of surfacing and manifesting in behavior that *can be seen*.

People will show sympathy for somebody who has black eyes and broken arms—"Oh, come over to my house. I'll protect you. I'll take care of you. I don't want that to happen to you ever again."

But when it comes to someone who is being mentally abused, they don't quite understand why she is crying out. They respond with: "Well, your husband is such a good provider. He takes care of you and the children. You've got an absolutely beautiful home. What are you talking about, he's abusive? And if he actually is, you know, *God can heal him!*"

But there is more to a home than a physical environment. There is a mental and emotional environment—and let's not forget the spiritual environment, as well. And those environments can be very unhealthy, even deadly. But most people don't give much if any thought to that. And, going by what they see, they ask, "How can you be a godly woman if you walk away from that (you know, beautiful home, even nice clothes, a husband who provides for you)?"

And then their next question is automatically, "Who have you got in the background? Who are you seeing? What are you doing?" And the fingers start to point.

So you have mothers who become basket cases and can't even be there mentally and emotionally, let alone spiritually, for their children, who are being destroyed by the dysfunction in the home. The wife sticks with a husband who finally becomes transformed on his death bed into the man of God he should have been all along, and then at the wife's funeral she is applauded for having stuck with her man (despite all his abuse, though this is not mentioned at the time). But back in the gathering of family and friends in that funeral setting sits the children of that couple—one has gone from one wreck of a marriage to another; the other is a blooming drug addict—lost as a goose in a snowstorm. The children's lives have turned into disasters, and they are the ones who are raising the grandchildren!

I know God works miracles, but I also know that God gives people a free will. Believing for wholeness in a mate is not to be done at the expense of losing your life and those of your children. And I'm not convinced that the situation has to reach the point of being physically life-threatening. There can be worse prisons that people have found themselves in than death itself. That's why I believe many choose suicide over staying in the "hell on earth" that has become their lot in life.

Some situations have called for the abused mate to walk out, rescuing the children and herself and still trusting God to make a way to bring wholeness to the abuser. God knows how to bring *others* across the path of the abuser to get him the help he needs.

I realize there are so many things to consider in these situations and that every situation is different. But the fact of the matter is that Christian theology has an awesome responsibility on its shoulders to deal with the issue of abuse in all its forms, as spirituality does engage the whole person—spirit, soul, and body. And when it comes to marriage, I agree with those in Christian theology who have supported Gernert's stance that "infidelity in marriage…is more than sexual unfaithfulness….It is acting in disloyalty and betrayal. In this way, abuse demonstrates infidelity."[7] Failure to recognize this has caused way too many victims of marital abuse to see no way out.

PART II

HE WAS THERE ALL THE TIME

Chapter 3

CONFUSED ABOUT CHURCH

FOR ALL PRACTICAL purposes I was left home *alone* when my mother died. I was a victim of abuse, convinced that I was unworthy, undesirable, and unwanted—because my own father had impressed this upon me many times. Oh, I wondered, *How could a just God take my mommy and leave my daddy, when I needed my mommy so very much?*

I hadn't been raised to know the Lord and to go to church. Mother did get saved just prior to her death, and someone told me she got filled with the Holy Ghost and danced all over the place about a week before she died. That just thrilled me! And then Dad came to know the Lord about a year and a half before he died. He got saved during the sickness that resulted in his death.

But neither Mother nor Dad took my sister and me to church up to the time of Mom's death, though Dad did take us to church for a while after that—but it didn't last. Then I went to church on my own, taking Barbara with me. It was a little place of worship close enough to walk to, though we had to cross a major thoroughfare getting there, making it a dangerous situation. And then Barbara and I went with Grandpaw to his church, to the one he attended and actually helped found. But that left me really confused about church and God, especially after having attended a different church before this one. It was a *very* different denomination from Grandpaw's, and it was all *really* confusing to me.

Then I got saved when I was about nine. Well, I don't know that I was saved; I can't really say that I was. But after that time I always said that I was because this certain lady in the church said so. But it was soon after Mother died. She died in September, and this was around Christmastime of the same year.

Grandpaw's church was putting on a Christmas program, and I went with him to see it. Grandpaw, from what I remember, had gone up to sing in the choir; and I was left sitting on the pew by myself.

And the choir was singing, "Away in the manger, no crib for a bed..." It was just so sad to me because I was sitting there without my mother, and I was missing her badly. It had only been about three months since she died, and the Christmas songs were making me sad. I had begun to cry. And instead of coming up and putting her arms around me and hugging me, this little lady with her hair in an up-do and her dress down to her ankles came over to me and asked, "What's the matter, hon'? You under conviction?"

I just shrugged my shoulders. I didn't know what conviction was. I can't say that she knew that my mother had passed away not too long ago. I would think she knew that it was Grandpaw's daughter that had died and that I was Grandpaw's granddaughter. But I can't say for sure.

But I was just sitting there crying, practically crying my face off; and she asked, "You under conviction?" And I didn't know what conviction was.

And then the preacher at some point talked about how bad hell was. I became really frightened, and thought, "Could there really be a place worse than where I live?" I just knew that if it was worse, I had to do whatever I could to keep from going there.

Crying over missing my mother, frightened by the thought of going to hell, and being tugged at by this little lady asking me, "You under conviction?" and then telling me, "Well, you need to go down to the altar and pray," I totally gave in to what this woman thought I should do. She grabbed me by the arm and down to the altar we went.

She said, "You're just under conviction. You need to get saved." And she added, "You just need to pray."

I didn't really know how to pray. I mean, I had talked to God before. I remember praying whenever I found Mother dead, "Please don't let my mommy be dead. Please don't let my mommy be dead. God, please don't let her be dead." And even when I was trying to find someone to help me after I found her, I prayed. But now I didn't know *what* this lady who had led me to the altar wanted me to pray. I didn't honestly know what she had in mind.

But I knelt at the altar and made an attempt to talk to God. "Lord, I'm... You know, I'm sorry..." I said a little bit of this and a little bit of that, and I just prayed all I knew to pray; and I especially asked God to save me from hell.

In a few minutes, the lady said, "Well, you're saved!"

I remember how everyone was quick to tell me all the things I shouldn't do if I wanted to go to heaven. No one told me about the love of Jesus and how He would always be right there with me. I still thought of God as that big God out there somewhere who oversaw everything and ran the world, and a God who particularly watched to see if anyone did anything wrong.

When Mama died, somebody gave me a little gold cross. Other than that, I didn't own any jewelry at all. My family had practically nothing—even went hungry at times. So that little cross was really special and meant a lot to me. Well, after I went down front that night to get saved, the lady who had stayed right with me through it all came and sat down beside me, and she said, "You'll have to quit wearing that little cross. And you can't get your hair cut. And you can't wear any makeup. And you have to wear your dresses a certain length."

And I remember thinking, *What did I do? What just happened to me?*

Nobody told me about the love of Jesus that night, and I sure needed to know about the love of Jesus right then. I just needed somebody, *anybody*, to put his or her arm around me and love on me. But I was left thinking, *I must be saved, because this lady told me I was. And she told me I couldn't do all that stuff. I guess that means I am saved; but I don't know how I got there.*

But I professed from then on that I was saved, but I'm not sure I was. I do know that the only time I felt any kind of happiness was when I would go to church, but I really didn't know why. I always prayed God would save my dad and just maybe he would quit drinking and be better to me—or maybe God would just let one of us, him or me, die. It would be many years later, after I became an adult, that I would go back to that same church and be pointed to God in a tremendously impacting way.

Chapter 4

THE BANTY HEN AND HER CHICKS

GAIN, IF ONLY someone in that church service that night had put his or her arm around me—that little nine-year-old who had lost her mother, her very world—and told me how much Jesus loved me, oh, how it would have spared me some terrible, near fatal times that lay up ahead.

Somehow I wonder if God Himself was not trying to get the message of His love across to me through some of my pets. After all, He used a donkey to speak to Balaam and a rooster to get a message across to Peter. He used the birds of the air and how He cared for them to show us how He would care for us.

God is a pursuing God and has a way of cutting through all the confusion and clutter to make things so simple and clear. And sometimes a little animal can communicate His pursuit of us like a human being can't. Sometimes an animal can be trusted when there are grave trust issues where human beings are concerned.

There is a real-life story along this line about how Jesus pursued an alcoholic and cocaine addict named Anne—a woman who was losing her best friend to cancer and whose promiscuity had culminated just that very week in the abortion of her child. Disgusted, abhorred, and saddened by what she had become, bleeding and weakened from the abortion, immersing herself in alcohol and drugs, she capped off the night with one last cigarette; and in her own words:

> After a while, as I lay there, I became aware of someone with me, hunkered down in the corner, and I just assumed it was my father, whose presence I had felt over the years when I was frightened and alone. The feeling was so strong that I actually turned on the light for a moment to make sure no one was there—of course, there wasn't. But after a while, in the dark again, I knew beyond any doubt that it was Jesus. I felt him as surely as I feel my dog lying nearby as I write this. And I was appalled....I thought about what everyone would think of me if I became a Christian, and it seemed an utterly impossible thing that simply could not be allowed to happen. I turned to the wall and said out loud, "I would rather die."

14

I felt him just sitting there on his haunches in the corner of my sleeping loft, watching me with patience and love, and I squinched my eyes shut, but that didn't help because that's not what I was seeing him with.

Finally I fell asleep, and in the morning, he was gone.

This experience spooked me badly, but I thought it was just an apparition, born of fear and self-loathing and booze and loss of blood. But then everywhere I went, I had the feeling that a little cat was following me, wanting me to reach down and pick it up, wanting me to open the door and let it in. But I knew what would happen; you let a cat in one time, give it a little milk, and then it stays forever....[1]

Anne would occasionally visit a certain church, situating herself in the rear of the building, listening to the singing, and then leaving before the message was preached. But a week after the unusual night when she sensed the presence of Jesus, while enduring the disagreeable aftereffects of drunkenness, she returned to that church, and this time remained for the sermon, which she found to be "so ridiculous, like someone trying to convince me of the existence of extraterrestrials." But then:

The last song was so deep and raw and pure that I could not escape. It was as if the people were singing in between the notes, weeping and joyful at the same time, and I felt like their voices or *something* was rocking me in its bosom, holding me like a scared kid, and I opened up to that feeling—and it washed over me.

I began to cry and left before the benediction, and I raced home and felt the little cat running along at my heels, and I walked down the dock past dozens of potted flowers, under a sky as blue as one of God's own dreams, and I opened the door to my houseboat, and I stood there a minute, and then I hung my head and said..."I quit." I took a long deep breath and said out loud, "All right. You can come in."[2]

Someone who couldn't imagine the likes of herself becoming a Christian, someone who felt rejected by others and even despised by herself, someone who was very much alone, except for her dog and having the feel of it lying nearby—Jesus communicated His love, desire, and pursuit of this someone in a very real, non-threatening way through a little animal, a cat, "following me, wanting me to reach down and pick it up, wanting me to open the door and let it in....the little cat running along at my heels."

And as a little girl, I believe Jesus was trying to communicate to me through my little pets that He was there—loving and desiring and pursuing me. He wanted me to have this understanding and relationship with Him, and especially for the road that lay ahead.

Someone had given me a banty hen and a banty rooster—the cutest little black and white creatures. And the mother hen had some baby chicks. And they, as well, were the cutest little things. I followed these special creatures around so much that I came to recognize that if danger came—such as the dog coming around or a storm approaching—the banty hen would cluck a certain way, and when she did, those little banty chicks would come running. The mother would hold out her wings, and all those tiny chicks would come running to get under them. And if there was still one chick straying out there, the mother would keep clucking until that one would come and get under her wing. She would then snuggle her babies close to her body, as intermittently they would poke their teeny heads through her feathers to take a peek at what was happening. Those babies knew not to leave the safety of their mother's wings, even though they were compelled to peek out when they could.

Today I understand that our Father God, my Papa, is like that toward us—wanting to gather us under His wings, just like that mother hen would gather her little brood under hers to provide safety during the storms. Her chicks wouldn't get wet as they snuggled under her wings.

The Ninety-First Psalm speaks of abiding or resting "in the shadow of the Almighty," of how "he will cover you with his feathers, and under his wings you will find refuge" (vv. 1, 4). Our Papa wants to be close to us; He wants to gather us up to His bosom just like we would embrace a little child who's skinned his knee. He just wants to say, "It'll be alright, darling; it'll be OK! I'll make it OK!"

> You will not fear the terror of night, nor the arrow that flies by day, nor the pestilence that stalks in the darkness, nor the plague that destroys at midday.... For he will command his angels concerning you to guard you in all your ways; they will lift you up in their hands, so that you will not strike your foot against a stone.
>
> —PSALM 91:5–6, 11–12

Just like we would for any one of our children or even a little animal that gets hurt, our God wants the very best for us. If a bird falls out of a tree, we want to scoop it up and blow air back into it—*whhhhhh*—and make it breathe again. As a small child, I found a bird that fell out of a nest; and I remember blowing, blowing, and blowing air into its beak. And in a few minutes, it raised its head up and started looking for its mama. I found its nest and put it back so its mama could find it.

And that's exactly how our Father feels about us. He's so tender and loving and caring. There's nothing like being in the presence of the almighty God, who stoops down and picks up a little sparrow and puts it back in the nest!

> Look at the birds of the air; they do not sow or reap or store away in barns, and yet your heavenly Father feeds them. Are you not much more valuable than they?
>
> —MATTHEW 6:26

He loves and cares for us that much.

There was to be more than one occasion in the days to come when God would literally breathe life back into me, *and I would live*. Just like I did that small bird—I breathed air back into its tiny beak, *and it lived*.

And that is exactly what happened to me at that all-important moment when I received of God's very Spirit—His breath of eternal life—and I was born again. We do not truly live until we have been infused with the Spirit of the living God. That's when we truly come alive in our own spirit. It would be many years later when as an adult I would actually have an awareness of this taking place in my life. Like I have said, I cannot say that this did not happen at that altar when I was nine years old, but not knowing what happened to me left me, through ignorance, to continue my life as usual, not enjoying this new life, including the privileges and benefits of a personal relationship with the God of the universe who, through the new birth, had become my Father.

Chapter 5

CREATED FOR LOVE

N O ONE HAD really told me about the love of Jesus. And my idea of God had not changed. I still saw Him overseeing the world, ready to crack His whip at the first sign of any wrongdoing. If only I had understood that God's main purpose for creating human beings was to have a family that He could love, rather than a people who would obey Him. God does seek our obedience but only because He knows what is best for us; after all, He created us. But not only does He know what's best for us, He actually wants the very best for us. But God, more than obedience (which is for our own good), wants a family to love, and then a family that will choose to love Him back. God loves first!

So I was created, first of all, to be loved by the God of the universe—and like a father loves a child. Created to be loved—fathom that! And secondly, I was created to love Him back, and then, only if I choose to do so. Oh, what a different picture of God this is than most see!

Too often the real problem down here on Earth is made out to be the human race's lack of power to be good, to do good—not to sin. But the real problem is a love problem. Not knowing how much we are loved by God, we can spend all of our lives trying to earn it when, in truth, finding security in God's love is what will actually destroy sin's power over our lives.

This is so far removed from the thinking that it's all about obeying God. Or the thinking that it is all about sin-management. Or the thinking that holiness is the ultimate goal. Obedience is important. And sin is evil and can lead to defeat and destruction. And God *is* a holy God. But what our very purpose for existence is really about is relationship, relationship with a heavenly Father who wants to share all of His riches with us, who does not want us to grovel at His feet but to sit with Him in heavenly places. (See Ephesians 2:6, KJV.)

Spirituality is not a formula; it is not a test. It is a relationship. Yaconelli writes:

> Spirituality is not about competency; it is about intimacy. Spirituality is not about perfection; it is about connection. The way of the spiritual life begins where we are *now* in the mess of our lives. Accepting the reality of our broken, flawed lives is the beginning of

spirituality not because the spiritual life will remove our flaws but because we let go of seeking perfection and, instead, seek God, the one who is present in the tangledness of our lives. Spirituality is not about being fixed; it is about God's being present in the mess of our unfixedness.[1]

How far removed the message of God's love is from the majority of people's thinking *that God is chasing them down to punish them*—that He is angry at them. Rather than understanding His desire to be a loving Father, all they can see is a terrible Judge coming after them. Fear of judgment might cause someone to run to God, but having a relationship of love with Him will cause us to experience more power and joy and righteousness than fear ever could. God both knows and desires this very thing! He doesn't want to use fear to coerce us into loving and obeying Him.

And then, along the same line, how far removed is the message of God's love from the majority of people's thinking that God is first and foremost out to be worshiped by us all. The daughter of famous missionaries T. L. and Daisy Osborn shared the understanding she and her family had of God, an understanding that was key to the success the entire family had on the mission field—a family of whom it is said that they have witnessed more physical healing miracles than any family that has ever lived. In an interview, she said, and I quote:

> We minister to hurting people like beggars that smell, with flies swarming around the—of no value to society, to their families, to themselves. But we see them as so precious to God—the fingerprint of God is on each one; and His whole desire is for their sake. This makes for such a different view of God than His just wanting people to worship Him…as though everything God made was so that He could be stroked. That is such a narcissistic idea of who He is![2]

And in case the meaning of narcissism is not clear to some, it has to do with "inordinate fascination with oneself," including extreme love of and satisfaction that comes from admiring oneself.[3] How far removed that is from who God is, as if He is interested in displaying His awesome magnificence to make us feel small and bow at His feet!

And another great fallacy when it comes to who God is has to do with the majority of people's thinking that God runs from our sin and messes—that He is so holy that He can't look upon our sin. Well, I've got news for you: when Adam and Eve sinned in the Garden, choosing to rebel against God and to do things their way, God didn't run from their sin. He actually showed up to be with Adam and Eve—and He wasn't raving and ranting mad when He did so. He showed up just like Jesus showed up for the woman at the well or Zacchaeus, the publican, or Matthew, the tax collector, or the woman caught in adultery.

God doesn't run from sinful humanity, and the church shouldn't either. Wayne Jacobsen explains:

> He didn't hide from Adam and Eve in the Garden. *They* hid from him as *he* sought them out. It is not that God cannot bear to look on sin, but that we in our sin can't bear to look on God. He's not the one who hides. We are. God is powerful enough to look on sin and be untainted by it. He has always done so. He did so at the cross.[4]

Struggling as a little girl feeling all alone in the world, being abused by none other than members of my own family, and holding myself responsible for that abuse—oh, if only I had known God at that time as someone who didn't see me as being undesirable like those around me did! Oh, if only I had known God at that time as someone who was eager and ready to run *into* my mess—not *away* from it—whether I had caused it or not! Oh, if only I had known Him as one who "longed to gather [His] children together, as a hen gathers her chicks under her wings" (Matt. 23:37), I would have known as a little girl that He was trying to say something *to me* about how much He was there *for me* as I watched that little banty hen and her chicks that I so much adored. But I didn't. And the worst was yet to come.

PART III

VALLEYS OF THE
SHADOW OF DEATH

Chapter 6

JUST SEE HOW BAD YOU DON'T NEED ME

HAD I BEEN told that December night I supposedly got saved that this is what the message of salvation was all about—that through Jesus Christ I came to know God as my Father, a Father who would never leave me nor forsake me, who cared for me like I had seen that banty hen care for her chicks, and even more, that I was valuable, I was worth Jesus going to the cross for me—one little girl would have been spared a lot of hurt. But, as it was, taking that lady's word that I had gotten saved didn't do a thing to change my thinking that I was doing something to cause the abuse I was experiencing—mostly from family members—since my mother's death.

I was just a kid and I had no mom. I may have become a new creature in my spirit while kneeling at that altar, but I did not automatically become transformed in my thinking. My mind was not renewed to the new life I had taken on, to the new creature I had become in my spirit. You can have something valuable, but if you don't know you have it you won't enjoy it. I didn't know the truth about my heavenly Papa, and therefore I didn't recognize the lies I believed about who He was and who I was in His eyes. If only I had known who I was in my Father's eyes!

Because I didn't, the abuse by family continued. I had to run and hide in the woods more times than I care to think about. The feelings of being unwanted, unloved, worthless, and so *very* alone were growing beyond the capacity I had to deal with them. I longed for my mother and my other loved ones who were in heaven. I felt like I could take it no longer. I felt powerless to change my situation. There was nowhere else to go. So I tried to take my life. I tried to commit suicide—not once but twice.

The first time I took a bottle of aspirin—a 150-count bottle of aspirin. I had heard about somebody doing that and it killing them, so I thought, "Hmmm, that's what I can do." And I took the whole bottle—all 150 pills—and it didn't kill me. It just made me sick. I was so upset by the fact that I didn't die. Nobody knew about this at the time; I didn't tell anybody—which is to dispute the automatic assumption of some that a suicide attempt is always for the express purpose of getting attention. Nobody ever knew—not for years to come—that I took those pills. I just regurgitated them and was furious that I didn't die.

And then the next time around I thought, "Well, that didn't work, so I will take everything in the house that looks like medicine!" Once more, getting attention and pity from others wasn't on my mind; I meant business. And I did—I took everything in the house that looked like medicine. I filled up both sides of the kitchen sink with medicine bottles, with everything in the house of the nature of prescription medicines, laxatives, and cough remedies. Anything that looked like medicine, I took it. I emptied *every* bottle in the house.

I had just taken a cussin' from Daddy for about the last time I could stand it. His words had knocked the remaining puff of wind that I had in my sail right out to sea. I'd had it; I couldn't do anything to please him. If I had supper on the table, it wasn't something he liked or it wasn't cooked right. If I didn't have it on the table right when he wanted it to be, I was in trouble. If I was still cooking it when he wanted it already done, I was in trouble. If it was cold, I was in trouble. And if he came in and I wasn't working on supper and was doing my homework, he'd throw my books across the floor and say, "Don't ever let me come in and catch you with your nose in those books again and without any supper on the table." And if he had trouble putting his legs in his pants—because I hadn't starched them enough to please him—he'd wad his pants up and throw them against the wall.

I could have cleaned the hardwood floors all day long and gotten down on my hands and knees to polish them with Johnson paste wax and then buffed them, and in my dad would come with drunks. He'd bring his drinking buddies in, and they would pour beer out onto the floor and say, "Ahhh, somebody's going to have to clean this up!" And I was just a kid of about twelve or thirteen—*just a kid*.

And then my little sister had said to me, "Me and my daddy don't need you." I loved my sister, but she was young and caught in the middle. It wasn't her fault, but I had taken more than I could handle of Dad's verbal abuse because of her.

So I said to myself, "Well, you just see how bad you don't need me." So I took all those medicines—*every* bottle in the house that I could find, and the neighbors found me passed out in the floor in front of the kitchen sink. And they were afraid of Daddy. They were afraid to take me to the hospital because they were afraid of what he would do. And so they took me and put me in their bed; that's the only thing they knew to do.

When I awoke from that suicide attempt, I was *furiously* angry that I was still alive. And from a natural perspective, I shouldn't have been—alive, that is. I shouldn't have survived the first attempt when I took a whole bottle of aspirins. And I surely shouldn't have survived this second attempt.

When my dad finally arrived at the neighbors' house where I was, he stood in their bedroom doorway, leaned on and propped his arm up against the door, and said, "Thought that was cute, didn't you! You try it again, and I'll beat the hell out of you!" After that, while I stayed at the neighbors until I got better, he *never* came to see about me, to see if I was OK.

All I can say is that God had mercy on this young girl and kept her for such a time as this. He did.

Chapter 7

UNDERSTANDING SUICIDE

IN LATER YEARS, I was to have my life horribly gripped by the suicide attempts of two people closely connected to me. *Successful* suicide attempts, these were. One was that of my stepdaughter and the other was that of my sons' father.

I am well aware of how suicide is viewed without reservation by many as the most cold-hearted, selfish act that anybody can commit—as cruelly leaving behind devastated loved ones and as blatantly offending God in displaying total disregard for the sanctity of the life He has given. When news of the tragedy is heard, heads began to shake, and the comment is voiced or else thought inwardly, "How could they?"

Suicide can be an intentional, selfish act—but not most likely. And while suicide itself is the intentional causing of one's death, there are a whole host of reasons why someone would do such a thing—reasons such as depression, despair, some underlying mental disorder, alcoholism, drug abuse, and financial difficulties; mental, physical, and sexual abuse; and various troubles with interpersonal relationships. The list goes on and on.[1] I am convinced that many deaths that were deemed suicides were not suicides at all but instead someone merely drinking and drugging himself into forgetfulness with no intention of actually overdosing and killing himself.

I've been there, having attempted to take my life twice. I know how low you can get; I know why a person would commit that act. And you can do it in an instant, on the spur of the moment, because things have seemingly got that bad for you at that moment in time—*really* that bad! And it's quite possible that at that moment the suicidal individual is not thinking about whom he (or she) is leaving behind and what heartaches will be dumped on them.

He is just thinking of a way out. He is convinced that he can't deal with his situation or situations anymore and that suicide is the *only* way to end it all. That's as far as this person is somehow able to see. He ceases to look ahead any further than that. He's not thinking about who is going to be hurt by what he's going to do or how bad they are going to be hurt. He is not thinking about the consequences; he is just thinking about ending the hurt.

I had come to the place that I thought life was unbearable, that I could no longer live. It was painful beyond description. I have walked through that valley where death seems the only way out. *I know.*

And I'm here today as living proof that you can overcome, no matter how bad things get—not because I survived two suicide attempts, since I had nothing to do with that. But I did survive feeling more worthless afterward than I did when going into the suicides; and I survived all the things that came after that, including divorce, five vehicle accidents, a head injury, a doctor's negligence, the flesh-eating disease, major heart surgery, and so on.

And today, as a result of surviving those tragic times, I am able to help many others who are coming down the same roads. It's called redeeming what the enemy wanted to turn into a disaster. Today, because of where I've been, I recognize those suicide symptoms. I recognize those who are merely holding on and hardly able to do so much longer. I've been there. I've walked in those shoes. *I know.*

Today I am a grandmother. I have a thriving pottery business. I have been positioned to touch people's lives by the multiplied thousands, even hundreds of thousands. This book would never have happened had I succeeded in ending my life either one of the times I attempted to do so. And I would like to get the message to everyone who would want to take his or her life—just go somewhere, get ahold of somebody, even if it's a rank stranger. Just get ahold of somebody who can help you get through that moment, because it's just a moment. It's not forever. And no matter how bad it is, it's not really as bad as you perceive it to be. Your imagination will make you think that it's a whole lot worse than it really is.

There my stepdaughter was—she had of recent buried both her grandmother and her mother within a year of each other due to cancer, and she had then received an unfavorable doctor's report herself. While in Mississippi—a state with zero tolerance for DUI's—she had been ticketed and was facing a hearing that she knew would lead to some jail time. Suicide was her way of dealing with all of this.

If only time and space would permit, story after story could be shared of those among the ranks of the unknown and even among the ranks of the world-renowned who faced a jail sentence and who did not allow their incarceration to have the last word. Instead, they took their lemon of a sentence and turned it into lemonade, making a comeback that resulted in an even better life than they had experienced before jail time. Some used their jail time as an occasion to advance their formal education. Some even turned their jail time into a season of helping others who were incarcerated rather than focusing on their own dilemma.

What if they had allowed the threat of a jail sentence to cause them to end it all? What if they had allowed themselves to think that going to jail was the end of the road? My stepdaughter was looking at going to jail for only a few days—that's *all* she was looking at. Granted there were things bothering her that had led to her DUI and dreaded jail time, but it was the threat of jail that became the decision-maker for her—the straw that broke the camel's back.

There is the story about the two fellows who both were divorced by their wives. One committed suicide, but the other wrote a "Somebody Done Me Wrong" song and became rich and famous. It's not what happens to you but how you react to it. But there are those who have lost all hope and feel hopelessly unable to react in any hopeful way. Yet somewhere in that seemingly bottomless pit of despair is still the possibility of making a right choice and seeing tragedy turned into triumph.

What it all boils down to is that the person who commits suicide somehow has lost his or her sense of self-worth—so much so that he sees no hope of anyone coming to his rescue, so much so that he sees himself better off dead. But when our value to God is recognized, the value others and even the value we place on ourselves pales in comparison and will not be allowed to push us to quit.

Again, it is a love problem—not knowing how much we are loved by God. And then, once we know how much we are loved by Him, we must not lose sight of that love and its great depth as we face hardship and trials.

If we can ever get a revelation of His love for us, that it's the kind of love that when we mess up, God wants to enter into our mess and save us, then fear and despair and failure and loneliness and rejection will no longer maintain their grip on us.

This kind of love gives us a reason for keeping on and succeeding *every* time—a reason that will empower us in a way that all the self-help books and seminars and financial resources and support groups and education and talents in the world could never do, and a reason that will empower us in a way that the *lack* of any and all of these will *never* keep us from succeeding.

We are loved by God. We are loved by God. We are loved by God. And so Romans 8:31-35, 37 is ours to shout from the mountaintop:

> If God is for us, who can be against us? He who did not spare his own Son, but gave him up for us all—how will he not also, along with him, graciously give us all things? [And that includes strength in our time of weakness.] Who will bring any charge against those whom God has chosen? It is God who justifies. Who is he that condemns? Christ Jesus, who died—more than that, who was raised to life—is at the right hand of God and is also interceding for us. [Now that's a picture to keep before us when we think we are all alone.] Who shall separate us from the love of Christ? Shall trouble

or hardship or persecution or famine or nakedness or danger or sword?...No, in all these things we are more than conquerors through him who loved us.

"Through him who loved us"—we are loved, and unconditionally, by God!

The truth is that if we are experiencing problems in a certain area over and over, it most likely is an ignorance problem and not a sin problem. And the biggest ignorance problem on the face of the earth today is in regard to the nature of God and His love. But two suicide attempts later—and miraculously surviving both—I still didn't know this. So my story continued to get worse. I committed yet another kind of suicide—*I got married at fourteen.*

Chapter 8

ANOTHER KIND OF SUICIDE

MIND YOU, I had been abused those years after Mother died, and I was really just a child. So, fitting right in with Southern tradition, I married at fourteen. But after eight years of marriage and giving birth to two children, I was divorced at twenty-two.

I was truly in love with my first husband. He had come back from serving in the military, and we started attending church together. *We were just trying to live at the foot of the cross*—that's what I thought. Now, I had been baptized before, but we, my husband and I, decided that we wanted to be baptized at the same time and join the church. And so the preacher laid us down on his arm, together, at the same time, and submerged us, together, at the same time—baptizing us simultaneously. I am emphasizing what I saw to be our *togetherness.*

I was the happiest little girl that ever could be. I thought that was the most wonderful thing—getting baptized together and joining the church. Why, a marriage based like that, with that kind of foundation, would just have to last forever! And talk about feeling like some fairy princess—I did. I had been blessed with two beautiful, healthy sons, and every Sunday morning I was dressing my little boys and taking them to church.

And then their daddy quit going to church with me. Quite suddenly, he just quit going to church with me. And I came to find out that this was when he was fooling around with his little girlfriend. It wasn't six months after we were baptized together that he brought a girlfriend home and told me he was in love with her and "there wasn't anything anybody could do about it."

And talking about somebody's little world come crashing down, *I thought I would die.* I truly thought I would die of heartbreak. Betrayed and rejected, my life came crashing down. Devastated, I went into some kind of crazy shock for two days. My husband told me later that he slapped my face and tried everything to snap me out of it. He said that I would get up and take care of the babies, go to the bathroom, and do whatever else I needed to do, and then I would sit back down...and stare. Looking back on this, I honestly believe that God allowed me to go into some kind of crazy shock so I wouldn't feel the pain.

My baby was about three months old, and his brother was a little better than two years old. And I myself was close to nineteen. I wasn't divorced until around three years later, when I was about twenty-two. I had kicked my husband out initially but ended up staying with him for a while because I had never worked a job outside the home. And because I had quit school to marry him at fourteen, I didn't have an education to fall back on.

So, before I could actually divorce him, I needed to get a job so I could support my little family. I couldn't just walk away from him—not right then. I had no place to go. Dad wouldn't help me, even after I went to him and told him what my husband had done.

It wasn't long after the shocking news of my husband's betrayal and I had kicked him out that I asked my dad to go to the store to get one of my babies some medicine. He had a temperature of 104. It was Christmastime, snow was on the ground, and I didn't have any transportation. So I asked my dad if he would *please* go get the baby some medicine. He said, "Well, the best thing I can tell you to do is have your old man come back home." And he would not go get my baby some medicine. So I didn't feel I had any other choice but to let my husband come back. I didn't have a job. I had no money. And he wanted to come home.

But his girlfriend was our next-door neighbors' sixteen-year-old daughter. And they blamed me for his indiscretion with their daughter, for "letting" him do what he did. I hadn't had a clue that it was going on. We were going to church. We had been baptized together. We had joined the church. I was feeling like a fairy princess. I thought a marriage like this would last forever.

But the neighbors blamed me. And we had to move.

Chapter 9

WHEN I PASSED THROUGH THE WATERS

THERE IS A Scripture verse so intrinsically melodious, so beautifully and powerfully phrased, that it has been made into song. Had its words been watercolors, a most glorious rainbow the canvas would have portrayed. Had they been a sculptor's tools, a monument celebrating victory would have been carved. That verse is Isaiah 43:2—"When you pass through the waters, I will be with you; and when you pass through the rivers, they will not sweep over you. When you walk through the fire, you will not be burned; the flames will not set you ablaze."

Five times in my life I have had a brush with death in the water. And four of those times weren't ones of coming close to drowning; I drowned. If you're found lying on the bottom of a body of water, wouldn't you say that you drowned? Well, I was found lying on the bottom two times. And then another one of the five times I felt my spirit leave my body. I mean, I had an out-of-body experience.

The first time I drowned I was on an outing with my mother and dad. They had gone on a picnic and were doing some fishing. Mother had gone back to the car to get something and had left me lying on a pallet. I know I was too young to crawl off the pallet, because Mother would never have left me there if that had been possible.

Dad had gotten his fishhook hung in a tree and was up in that tree getting his hook unhung. And when he happened to look down there I was at the bottom of a cold mountain stream. Evidently I had rolled off the pallet and come to rest on the spine-chilling stream's rocky bed. And Daddy dove out of that tree to get me. The reason he had that day off from work was because he had the mumps. I'm surprised that today I have a baby sister, Barbara, because Dad dove into that water with the mumps.

But there I lay on the creek's bottom. Dad scooped me up and shook me; he shook the water right out of me—and I lived. My thinking is that if the drowning didn't get me that day, the hypothermia should have. It wasn't summertime, and I was just a baby, not even crawling yet.

The next time I drowned I was four years old. My family was in Florida with friends, and Mother and I were on some kind of inflatable float. We were lying across it on our tummies and riding the waves, and Mother said, "Scoot over a little."

And I remember thinking, "Hmm, I'm about to fall off as it is."

But what my mother had in mind was for me to scoot closer to her, not farther away. However, I scooted in the opposite direction. And about that time a wave hit us, and I fell off. I was caught in an undertow, and the undertow swept me up and then washed me out away from shore. Miraculously I was found when someone's feet hit against me on the ocean floor. It was Dad who found me once more, picked me up by the heels, and, yet again, shook the water out of me. I lived.

The next time I was about ten. This was after Mother died. I was waterskiing at a lake, and I love to ski on one ski, outrunning the boat. I was way out in front of the boat as it was circling around and around, allowing me to outrun it. And I fell. Now, the lake was quite deep. And I remember it being cold and dark and then continuing to get even colder and darker. I had fallen so hard that I knocked my ski belt down around my ankles, so I just kept going down, down, down, down, down, till I couldn't see anything anymore. While I was in that cold, dark deep, the boat that I was skiing behind went back to the bank to get the other boats—we had two other boats with us. Because I hadn't come back up, the others had gone back to get help. And while all three boats were driving around in search of me, I suddenly popped out of the water.

As I had sunk deeper and deeper, I had somehow got turned around and was heading back in the direction of the water's surface, and I saw a light. I kept going for the light, going for the light, going for the light, and just before I got to the light I opened my mouth. And that's when I seemed to take in half the lake. I came up spitting and sputtering.

The rest of the party was scared to death. I had been underwater for so long—long enough for them to go back to the bank and get the other boats—that they didn't think I would ever come back up. That's the third time I drowned.

The fourth time I was skiing with my husband and my son. The three of us were skiing when I hit a wave or a wave hit me, causing my ski to come off, fly up in the air, and come back down to hit me on the chest and knock me unconscious. My husband and son were unaware of this happening. I had dropped off behind them, leaving them ahead of me, and it was a long time before they realized I was gone. When they did, they came back looking for me, only to find me facedown in the water because that lick with the skis had deflated my lungs. When I had plunged facedown, my lungs had filled up with water.

I was taken back to the dock, an ambulance was called, and miraculously,

I was resuscitated, but all the cartilage was torn loose in my chest. That was the fourth time I drowned.

But there was yet another time. My sons, a daughter-in-law, and I were at the beach. Having driven all day, we just wanted to run out and get some waves. The boys had some one-man rafts; they would get on the front end of the rafts, and we girls would get on the back. We'd ride out on the waves, and then we'd ride back. And when we'd end up back at the shore, of course, the raft would capsize because of the undertow.

There again, we had an undertow; and we didn't know we were at the beach at the time of riptide and weren't supposed to be in the water. We hadn't paid any attention to certain flags and warnings that were posted. We made note of these later—a little too late.

So we had returned to shore several times, and our raft had flipped over each time. We just kept doing it—laughing and giggling, with no concern that there was any danger involved. Now my sons, both of whom had played football, at that time weighed about 215 pounds each. They were these big, husky guys. And my daughter-in-law Krissy and I were just tiny little things. She especially was just a little bitty thing, but I was quite small, as well, at the time. And the boys, riding on the front of the rafts, would land on top of us girls when our rafts would capsize. And that didn't present a problem until my son fell right on top of me, and I somehow got caught in the undertow.

This sent me spinning over and over and over, and the back of my head bouncing and bouncing and bouncing on the ocean bottom as I went. I kept banging my head on the ocean floor, and I couldn't get upright. I remember thinking, "I'm going to die right here. This is a strange way to go, but I guess it's OK."

I left my body and sensed traveling a good distance—above and beyond what was happening with my sons and daughter-in-law below. But then my youngest son saw an arm in the crashing waves.

He said later, "Mom, you looked like a helicopter. Every once in awhile I'd see a foot, and then every once in awhile I'd see an arm. And finally I saw an arm and was able to grab it."

My son grabbed me and yanked me—spitting and sputtering and thrashing about—out of the crashing and frothing waves. And when he yanked me out, my spirit went back into my body.

"Mom, we got to get you back to the room!" he stated.

And I said, "Oh, I'm not dead!" And I went right on having fun. When I passed through the waters, He was with me!

Chapter 10

THE DOOR OF DEATH

T<small>O THIS DAY</small>, not only do I not have one bit of fear of the water, but I do not have one bit of fear of death. If one is prepared to go to heaven to be with the Lord, dying is a most wonderful experience, and I want to pass this message on to others for the time of their departure or for a time when they may be with someone who is dying. If one is prepared to go to heaven, dying is a most exhilarating and liberating experience. You don't feel the weight of your body. You don't feel any worry. You don't have a care. You just feel the utmost peace and ecstasy as you simply move from this life to a greater life—*the greatest life*—an immortal, eternal life in the presence of the Lord.

And heaven is more than being in the presence of the Lord. It is a place, and then more. Life goes on there. Community goes on there. When the children of God die, they are not dead. They have just gone through a door called death, to a new place of residence called heaven. They don't live on Earth anymore. And they are very much alive!

There are those who believe that when someone dies, his or her spirit and soul remain in the body here on Earth, and then Jesus, at the Resurrection, returns to raise the dead. This is *not* what 1 Thessalonians 4:13–18 says.

> Brothers, we do not want you to be ignorant about those who fall asleep, or to grieve like the rest of men, who have no hope. We believe that Jesus died and rose again and so we believe that God will bring with Jesus those who have fallen asleep in him. According to the Lord's own word, we tell you that we who are still alive, who are left till the coming of the Lord, will certainly not precede those who have fallen asleep. For the Lord himself will come down from heaven, with a loud command, with the voice of the archangel and with the trumpet call of God, and the dead in Christ will rise first. After that, we who are still alive and are left will be caught up together with them in the clouds to meet the Lord in the air. And so we will be with the Lord forever. Therefore encourage each other with these words.

Paul tells us here that when Jesus returns, those who are asleep in Him (meaning those who were saved before they died)—who are "the dead in Christ"—"God will bring with Jesus." They will return *with* Him, implying that their soul and spirit are already in heaven with Jesus before He returns; otherwise He could not bring them *with* Him at the time of His second coming. That's why Paul can tell us that "to be away from the body" is to be "at home with the Lord" (2 Cor. 5:8).

So death becomes not about the finality of life here on Earth, but about the reality of life in heaven. You have no sadness about leaving your family behind; you don't have that kind of awareness of your family at that time. At that moment, you're only looking forward—you're not looking behind.

When I drowned and sensed my spirit leaving my body and was thinking that this was a strange way to go, I was aware that I was out of my body—way out and above my sons and daughter-in-law below. Now, what takes place to get you to that moment when your spirit leaves your body—the actual dying process—might not be so pleasant for some. It might involve suffering and pain, brought on by old age, accidents, sickness, and disease. But once you die, the pain is over.

There is a difference between the dying process and death, and we need to understand that. When we are told in Psalm 116:15 that "precious in the sight of the Lord is the death of his saints," it is not the dying process but death—the occasion of the saint of God leaving his body and entering the presence of the Lord—that is being referred to.

While the dying process may not be a positive experience, death for the child of God is. As for the death of a person who isn't saved, I shudder at the thought of it. I've heard stories. I had my uncle tell me all about his experience of going into the pits of hell once. He painted such a picture that I don't even want to think about it.

Chapter 11

TIRED OF BEING RUN OVER

"...in labours...in stripes...in prisons...in deaths oft"
—2 CORINTHIANS 11:23, KJV

I'M NOT SURE Apostle Paul had anything on me when it came to challenges and struggles. I haven't yet mentioned the six car accidents I was in, with one of these being a related-to-a-car accident, not a wreck. Actually it was a car accident that landed me in the pottery-making business—another one of those instances of taking what the enemy meant for harm and seeing it turned around for the good. But before that accident there were five others.

I would say that the worst of these vehicle accidents came at a time when I had just gotten out of the hospital with stomach ulcers. My son came to me and said, "Mom, I've just gotta go to school. I can't miss anymore school. Can you please get up and take me to school?"

Only the day before had I come home from the hospital, but I dragged myself out of bed like a good mama should and took my son across town to school. On my way back home, traveling on a four-lane highway, I had come to where I needed to make a left-hand turn onto another road. There was no turning lane into which to shift my car, so, turning my left-turn signal on, I sat in the left-hand lane for quite some time, waiting for the oncoming traffic to pass and the way to become clear.

Coming upon me in that same lane was a lady who was fooling with her kids, and she never even saw me until she hit me in the back end. She never even had time to apply her brakes. She just hit me full force, knocking me over into the lane to my left and positioning me to hit and be hit by another car head-on. Both of these cars—the one that rammed me and the one I rammed—were big cars, *and mine wasn't.*

My car was compressed like an accordion—*whammed* one way over into another lane, and then *whammed* another way by oncoming traffic. The first lick resulted in my arms and hands breaking the steering wheel in half. The second lick—the head-on collision—sent me flying, hips first, backward between my bucket seats, breaking off the backs of both front seats as I went. And when I came to, my body was twisted between what was left of those two seats. My face was pressed against the car's rear floorboard on the passenger side, my arms were pinned to my sides, and my toes were up under the dash on the steering wheel side.

The ambulance attendants who took me from the scene of the accident to the hospital later came to the hospital to see me, telling me that they hadn't expected me to make it. And the emergency room doctor came to visit me several times, having not expected, like the ambulance attendants, that I would survive.

He was not the doctor who was actually assigned to my case, so I asked, "Why do you keep coming to see me? You're not my doctor."

He replied, "I know. But I had two patients come in the same day, and I didn't think either one of you would live. But you were worse than the other one."

I asked, "Well, I know what happened to me, but what happened to the other guy?"

"Oh, he was hang gliding," he explained, "and slapped into the side of the mountain."

And then another time I was just sitting at a stop sign waiting for the traffic to pass so I could make a right-hand turn when this church bus came from my right and made a left-hand turn into the lane beside me on the left. But as the bus driver made his turn he turned too short, and the whole back end of the bus came up over the front of my car.

Now I was in a Camaro with a console between the bucket seats in the front. And when the bus's back left wheel came up over my car's hood and right up to the windshield, there was no place for me to go; there was no scooting over or back. I was pinned. And for some mysterious reason—you know, those seemingly coincidental times when God chooses to be anonymous—that wheel slid right past me and didn't come into the car on top of me. It went all the way across the front, right up to the windshield, and then back down the front end of the car to the left, totally missing me.

And another time, I was just a passenger. I had gone with a group of people up to a park in east Tennessee. We had Kool-Aid and sandwiches, and the guys played touch football. The guy I was with, however, slipped and fell while playing, landing against the wheel of his car. Seeing stars, he shook himself and continued to have fun with the rest of us for about another hour or so until we began our caravan back home in our string of Corvettes.

I was occupying myself with a tape, the kind that was used with an eight-track tape player, trying to pull the ribbon out and get it straightened so it would fit correctly back onto its reel, so I wasn't paying attention to the driving. I could hardly see over the dash as it was, being a short person and with Corvettes designed to leave you feeling like you're hunkered in some fox-hole. Slouched down in the seat and fooling with that tape, I wasn't aware that the guy driving our car was veering off the road, let alone that he was literally unconscious.

At the same time, another car was coming toward us head-on, and in an attempt to avoid a collision its driver was veering off the highway. But our car kept veering as well, to the same side of the highway. The oncoming driver got off the road, but we still hit him head-on on my side of the car and the passenger side of his car.

I remember thinking, "If we don't get stopped, it's going to kill us! We're going to get killed if we don't get stopped," because the other car kept coming.

The cars bounced off of each other after impact, and our car kept going. And I thought again, "We're going to die if we don't get stopped!" And I remember being aware of something seemingly coming up through the floor of the car—these stub-like things, but, in fact, my head had gone forward and down and had struck the apparatus for shifting gears—a rod-shaped instrument that had a metal protrusion on each side. My head had hit one of those metal protrusions twice. It hit it the first time when we smashed into the other vehicle head-on. After lunging forward and down and then back after that collision, I then lunged forward again—hitting the gear shift a second time with my head—when the wheel of our Corvette came off.

Here I was sitting in the floorboard of a Corvette, holding in my hands a big clump of hair and some white stuff. I thought the white stuff was a fragment of the Corvette's white fiberglass, but actually, it was a piece of my skull. And with every beating of my pulse, my blood would gush.

Gathering around the car, my friends were asking, "How are we going to get her out of there?"

And I answered, "Well, I can get out, but I need to put something on this cut. Has anybody got a rag that I can put on this cut?" I was in some kind of crazy shock. I asked, "Has anybody got a handkerchief, Kleenex, anything—you know, some rag I can put on this cut? I'm going to bleed to death." I just knew by the way my blood was gushing that an artery had been cut.

When somebody found a handkerchief I asked for help in placing it on my cut. When that person got close enough, he gasped, "Oh, my God, it doesn't matter! Just put it somewhere!"

I had to beg before somebody would actually grab hold of my hand and slap it onto the place where my head was gashed. I was then loaded into a van and taken nearby to a little ol' clinic. And I was left sitting on the table, wide awake, while my head was sewed up. The attending physician had told me that where my skull had been cracked open and a piece removed as a result of the accident, he could see clear through to my brain. However, he did not have the capability of repairing that damage and was only able to temporarily pull my scalp over the gaping wound.

I asked, "Before you put the bandages on, I want to take a look." There was a big, jagged scar. And with my hair being somewhat long, part of it was left that way while the rest was shaved. So when I looked at myself in the mirror, I said, "Well, I know how Frankenstein feels now."

On top of that, when the feeling started coming back in my head, I wasn't even given so much as an aspirin, and I was checked every fifteen minutes to keep me awake, because I obviously had a concussion. I wasn't allowed to sleep or to have anything for pain. And talk about dying. I thought I would die! I never had so much pain in all my life. By way of sticking needles into my head, I was given an anesthetic to numb the pain before sewing me up, but when my brain started swelling and the anesthetic wore off, *wheeeeewww!*

One time I was traveling down the road and watched as a Volkswagen full of people heading in my direction ran a stop sign and commenced to come all the way across four lanes. I moved over to give them a lane, but they kept coming on across. By the time I reached where they were, as my vehicle had continued to move, I hit them in the side. It wasn't my fault. None of the accidents I was in was my fault, not a single one.

In another incident, which wasn't actually a car accident, I was parked on the side of a hill holding something in my hands as I attempted to get into the car. A gust of wind caused the car door to close on my head, knocking me unconscious. And I laid there for several hours. That was another concussion.

I honestly got to the place that for a long time I couldn't drive, and if I had had a choice I probably would *never* have driven again. But I didn't have a choice. I had two boys. I had to take them to school. I had to go to work. I was holding down three and sometimes four jobs at a time. I was in my early twenties, and I had six accidents in a period of two to three years.

At the time I talked about and even kind of laughed about wanting to get a Sherman tank, paint it red, and loudly scream, "Here I am! Watch out! I don't want anybody hitting me anymore. I want all the protection around me I can get. I'm tired of people running over me."

PART IV

THERE IS ALWAYS A WAY

Chapter 12

PRICELESS BUT HARD

I was divorced. The boys' dad paid his child support when he wasn't on strike and laid off. But the strikes were occurring at least once a year and lasting months at a time, and my boys' dad never caught up any of his behind payments whenever he went back to work. He just started back up like no payments had been missed.

I was not only raising two boys, but my sister had come to live with me because our stepmother had threatened to kill her. Times were hard. I had to work even as many as four jobs to take care of my family. I worked on the assembly line building stoves. I would go home in the evening, paint my fingernails, and sell Mary Kay cosmetics. Back in those days, a Mary Kay representative had to do presentations or shows—three and four shows a week—where they did facials and demonstrated the products. You couldn't just sell the products like they do now. I'd go home and clean my nails and put on my good stuff. That made for my second job. And my third source of employment was a food store, working in the meat market on the weekends. And then my fourth job was making dried flower arrangements and placing them for sale in shops all over Chattanooga. I did this between two and four in the morning because that was when my boys were asleep. It was my spare time, the only time I had left.

Raising my boys was a highlight of my life, a priceless time—*but hard*. Spencer, the younger of the two, was the sweetest little child. People would say, "Oh, what a pretty little girl," even when he was dressed in a ball uniform and even though I got him a haircut when he was just a few months hold.

On the other hand, oh, brother, what a challenge he was! Hyper—into everything! At eighteen months to two years old, he climbed three steps to get onto the kitchen counter so he could reach my purse on top of the fridge, and he took my flu medication. *He ingested it.*

In addition, he was a firebird. He set a shoestring ablaze in a closet full of clothes. He started a bonfire in the carport beside the car tire that was next to the car's gas tank. He started a fire in the back seat floorboard of the car. I didn't smoke, and because of Spence I didn't keep matches in the house for any other reason. I didn't even acquire matches to light his candles for his birthday cake.

While in day care at four years old, my son, who was supposed to be in the basement of the church's three-story building, set fire to the toilet paper in the upstairs bathroom—resulting in a six-alarm fire. So, naturally, he was thrown out of day care, and I begged for him to be taken back. I was working four jobs; I needed to have him in daycare. He was either eating or drinking or doing something he shouldn't. It wasn't that I wasn't a good mother or that he wasn't a good child. He, actually, was a very good child, and he was brilliant—especially in the mechanical arena. When it came to mechanics, he could seemingly do anything and was willing to tackle anything.

Spence was also a charmer; teachers loved him. And I—I just wanted to love him on one hand and to kill him on the other (figuratively speaking, of course). I found out later that he neither heard nor saw well. And then later it was determined that he had a reading disorder; he was dyslexic, impairing his learning ability. He was placed at the back of his class because of mischievousness, and then he *really* couldn't see the board. He spent considerable time in the principal's office.

But, like I said, Spence was brilliant when it came to mechanics. Today he is an entrepreneur with two businesses of his very own—a landscape business with several employees and a packing and shipping business.

Philip, on the other hand, was not just a very good little boy; he was the *perfect* little boy—though he did at one time drink a bottle of aftershave, and I had to have his stomach pumped. Laughingly and jokingly, I have sometimes said, "If I had Spence first, there wouldn't have been a Phil." Phil's brilliance manifested in a different way from Spence's. In the second grade he authored his own little book. Today he works for himself as well—having two jobs, with the second one being a sports talk show host on the radio.

He literally invented a sports game when he was only nine to ten years old. He would sit and play and play and play that game until he perfected it. And when he became an adult, he got a patent on this game. I was so proud of him. How many kids invent a game when they're nine or ten years old? That's just the way his mind worked. He could lie on the floor on his stomach and do calculus, watch TV, and play that game—he could do all of those things at the same time.

He has such a quick mind and then such a dry sense of humor, to boot. I mean, he comes up with such witty, dry things that are so above me. He tells these jokes that I just don't get.

The year Phil graduated, his school won the state championship in football. And that was the greatest thing that had ever hit Valley Head, Alabama. I mean, we were just this little one-horse town; and the merchants even had to get together and build a proper field house for the opposing team and revamp the stadium, including renting stadium seats, to accommodate the state championship play-offs. The school didn't have money, so we merchants got together and raised the money to do all this. We were so proud of our team for winning the state championship; it was such a big thing for our town. And for my son Phil, being very sports-minded, that was a grand time in his life.

And after those athletes at Valley Head would get out of school, they would come into our grocery store, and Phil worked there. Those football players would come in to get Phil and their Cokes and refreshments and to celebrate. There wasn't any other place in town to go. I would fix them something to eat; the entire team were like my own boys. It was a rich and memorable time for me, my boys, and them.

Chapter 13

STANDING ON YOUR OWN TWO FEET

OTH OF MY boys helped me in the restaurant business—even while they were still young. Spence would get up in the early morning and help put on soup and chili and would come back after school and help close the business. Phil helped cut meat in the old-fashioned meat market.

I used to feel bad because my boys had to help me like that. But if you were to ask them today how they felt about all of this, they would tell you they didn't have it bad—that experiences like this helped prepare them for life.

I'd beat myself up thinking that I didn't give a lot of attention to those two, but Spence says today that I was always there when he needed me. He speaks out about this more than Phil, who doesn't like to talk much. Spence and I have been more communicative with each other down through the years than Phil and I—largely, I believe (and I say this laughingly, as well), because Spence was seemingly always in trouble and needed me more. I was always bailing him out of trouble.

I did make time to go on picnics with my boys and to take them fishing and hunting. I wanted them to grow up manly—to be men—yet I taught them how to cook and do laundry. I taught each of them that if his wife worked at a job and he arrived home from work before she did, then he was to put in a load of laundry and put supper on. If they expected their wives to share in making a living, then I taught them to help their wives at home. "I'd better not hear of you going home and lying on the couch if your wife comes in from work after you do. If she does, you help her do all the cooking and taking care of the children."

They've grown up being taught that this is what they should do. And I think it's wise to teach your boys to help at home. Just because they're boys doesn't mean they can't fix supper. Even if just because they live alone before they're married, they need to know how to cook. They need to know how to do laundry. If something were to happen to either of my boys' wives, my boys don't need to be in a position of not knowing how to take care of themselves. Everybody needs to know how to take care of themselves.

We simply live in a world where, unfortunately, too many think others are supposed to take care of them. And a primary reason for this is that the parents did not train their children to be responsible. They took care of them in areas they weren't supposed to, or else they continued doing things for their children when it was time for the children to step up to the plate and do them. They prompted and enabled laziness and selfishness, and that laziness and selfishness continued to manifest in the children's adult years. And then there is that element in the world that has been conditioned to want everything else—such as the government and the school system and even the church—to assume responsibility for their children.

You know, I was left essentially home alone at nine years old when my mother died, and I had to learn the hard way how to cook and take care of most everything. And then I was left by my children's father to be a single parent. So, I taught my boys early how to take care of themselves so that if something were to happen to me they could take care of themselves. That might sound morbid to some, but I wanted my boys to be able to stand on their own two feet— not to be left totally devastated if they were ever to be left on their own but to be able to take care of themselves.

They learned how to scramble eggs when they were just youngsters. They learned how to make a simple breakfast of scrambled eggs and toast, to make a sandwich for lunch, or to be able to take care of themselves in other ways. And many times I would have to call home and say, "Be sure to throw your uniform in the wash; you've got ball practice this evening."

Chapter 14

HAVING FUN WHILE MAKING
THE MOST OF THINGS

I TOOK MY BOYS to every single ball practice and ballgame. They played on two separate teams always, and we never missed a game. They played both football and baseball. Even when I worked all those jobs, up to four at a time, I still managed to take my boys to their practices and games, and I managed to go to every practice and every game.

I didn't have money to spare, but we did enjoyable things. In addition to fishing and hunting, I'd take them cave exploring. We'd go into caves and look for dinosaur bones. Our picnics were never just a picnic where we roasted hot dogs and marshmallows; they would always be an adventure. We'd always be scavenging, looking for something, and we'd have so much fun doing that.

Spence was telling me just the other day, "Mom, you just made that fun." We had next to no money to do anything extra, but I had a vivid imagination. God gave me a vivid imagination, so we just lived on that.

People have gotten so far from that. They grieve because they can't go out and buy their kids expensive Nintendo systems or whatever is popular today; or they feel like they've got to work to buy this and buy that—and they miss out on being *with* their kids and doing the things that don't cost anything but love and time. Love, time, and effort—those three things right there are free. They don't require money. But so many parents spend their time doing extra work to buy stuff that doesn't involve them being with their kids.

And my son was telling me, "Remember, Mom, when we went down to the park, and it was about to come up a storm? We had a kite in the sky, way, way up out of sight. We had kept adding string to it. And we had it way, way up, nearly out of sight, and a storm was coming. We were trying to get the kite reeled in, but we couldn't. Finally we just had to cut the line because the storm was coming, and we had to get out of the rain."

And he continued, "Oh, we hated cutting that string. We just hated cutting that string; but we had to, because we had to get out of the storm."

And I had actually forgotten about that occasion, but Spence remembered it so vividly. And he said, "But we had so much fun on that day with that kite."

And what did a kite cost? About $1.15 back in those days. But we only had one kite; I could only afford one kite with two boys. But we had a blast doing those kinds of things. And some days I would take Spence and Phil down to the farm, down to my grandpaw's farm. We, Grandpaw and I, would take them fishing in a little creek, and we would catch bream. Grandpaw and those two boys would bait their hooks, and as soon as their line would go into the water they would catch fish.

All three of them threw their fish out onto the bank, and my job was to chase the fish down, put them in the creel, and re-bait the hooks. I was running my legs off the whole time trying to keep up with those three as they caught their fish and left them flopping on the bank for me to grab hold of and put in the creel, and as they needed me to re-bait their hooks so they could do it again. Those boys got spoiled to the point that they thought that every time they went fishing the fish were supposed to be biting like that. Fishing at their grandpaw's was a part of their growing up days that they will never forget.

One of the first times I took my boys fishing, Spence caught a big ol' mud turtle. And when that thing came up out of the water with that big mouth agape, Spence threw his pole down! He didn't want to fish for a long time afterward for fear that he would catch a monster of some sort—which is what that mud turtle looked like to him. We had the biggest laugh about that!

I remembered that day well because I had caught a mud turtle like that when I was little, and I knew exactly how Spence felt. I had thrown down the fishing pole and gone running and screaming just like he did, so I could just feel his heart beating out of his chest as that big ol' monster face with that big mouth open wide came up out of the water. All you could see was that big mouth and big turtle cheeks.

Yes, I had fun with my boys; we made good memories together. But I tried, you know; I had to put forth the effort. I didn't always do everything right, but I was found trying. With what little time and what little money I had, I was found trying.

I must say that in the midst of all the sorrow that my boys and I have gone through—and we have had our fair share—we have a story of happiness in our home that most people who haven't even touched on the tragedies that we've endured have hardly begun to experience. I would say that most people have shared so very little in their kids' lives.

Think about it: If someone were to say, "My mother drowned five times, two of which were after we were born; was in six car accidents; has fought a deadly disease; has undergone major heart surgery; was divorced and had to raise us by herself; and so on," you might tend to think, What a horrific life these kids have lived! And, yet, in the midst of all our tragedy, my children, I would say, have been blessed with a richer upbringing than perhaps the majority of kids in the world. I am not boasting; I say that only to make the point that life can have wholeness in the midst of terrible things going on. As deep as the pain is, I believe that, conversely, the joy can be that high. Life can go on, can have meaning in the midst of all the things that we experience in this fallen world. And that makes for a very powerful story. My life may seem to have been full of tragedy, but make no mistake, it has also been full of triumphs.

You know, you can see the glass as half empty or half full. One person— a little boy—went as far as to say, "I don't even see the glass." Because *all* things can be turned around for our good, life doesn't have to be measured in terms of how much bad there is compared to how much good we have; life can be full, abundant no matter what the circumstances and no matter what resources we have available.

Chapter 15

GETTING RID OF THE VICTIM MENTALITY

I'VE BEEN TOLD that I could take a bushel basket and a piece of burlap sack and make a beautiful table out of it. And that's what I've always tried to do. And I don't boast about this either. I honestly see that this is what God has done with me—He has taken me with all my strengths and weaknesses, all my smartness and all my ignorance, all my accomplishments, and all my goof-ups, and not given up on making the best out of me. And with all of us having been created in the image of God, I honestly believe that's innate in us all, to take what we have and make the best out of it.

I just believe that we have let ourselves be sold a lie, even lots of them, and have allowed ourselves to be talked out of who we really are and what we really are capable of accomplishing in life. We listen to others' thoughts about us, and because we're not knowledgeable of the most important opinion in the world about us—God's, that of our Creator—we allow ourselves to think the thoughts of others without even examining them. We swallow their opinions and reasoning, not even questioning them. I am not saying that we should never listen to the thoughts and opinions of others; people can have some good, constructive things to say. But, we should never let others do our thinking for us or have the final word. God should have the final say-so.

We are told in Isaiah 58:7 (NKJV) to "not hide yourself from your own flesh." With that meaning that we are to not hide ourselves from the needs of our own flesh and blood, I think that includes not hiding ourselves from our own personal needs—as in, "Let's get real with ourselves!" We need to confront the lies, including the victimized attitudes that have resulted in how our lives are being lived. We must uproot them. Isaiah 54:17 tells us that "no weapon forged against you will prevail, and you will refute every tongue that accuses you. This is the heritage of the servants of the Lord, and this is their vindication from me." *The Message* Bible renders the latter part of this verse as, "This is what God's servants can expect. I'll see to it that everything works out for the best."

When we understand this about ourselves—that according to Jeremiah 29:11 a future of hope and prosperity is what God has planned for us, that this is not some desire of our heart that *dare we dream*, some good idea that we have come up with and hope God will go along with it—then taking what resources we have in this world and making the most and best out of them takes on new meaning. It is no longer simply something that we can and that would be nice to do, but it's who we are—what we are meant and empowered to be, to do, and to have—as being the creations of God.

It's time we examined what kind of thinking we are allowing to go on in our heads. "But if we [we, we, we] judged ourselves, we would not come under judgment" (1 Cor. 11:31): if we would only judge ourselves, not hiding ourselves from ourselves but examining the thinking that we are allowing to go on, then we would not have to suffer the penalty of the fruit that is being produced in our lives as a result of it.

> For as he [a man or woman] thinks in his heart, so is he.
> —PROVERBS 23:7, AMP

A gentleman by the name of Frank Outlaw summed the message of this verse up very well:

> Watch your thoughts; they become words.
>   Watch your words; they become actions.
>   Watch your actions; they become habits.
>   Watch your habits; they become character.
>   Watch your character; it becomes your destiny.[1]

Your thoughts become your destiny! That's why Apostle Paul tells us to cast down wrong-thinking. (See 2 Corinthians 10:5.)

I believe we can take any situation and turn it around for the good. I believe that message is at the root of God's plan of redemption. He's all about restoration. That's His nature, and that's our nature too.

We can't just allow life and its situations to do us in and rob both us and those we have the opportunity to affect of our destinies—situations like, "Well, I don't have this...," or "I don't have that...," or "If only my husband would...," or "If only my children wouldn't...," or "If only my dad hadn't...," or "If only my past hadn't been...," or "If only the economy was...," or "If only the government could..." We can "own" our destinies, or we can turn them over to fate and circumstances, our spouse, our children, our parents, our past, the economy, or the government.

When two paying jobs weren't enough to make ends meet, I just got another job. I didn't stop to say, "If somebody doesn't help me, I can't make it." More times than one there wasn't anybody to help me.

There is a world of people who have put their lives on hold because they're waiting for some certain something to happen, as in for certain resources to come their way or for someone to give them something or for someone to do something for them. We can wait and wait for that certain something to happen, for circumstances to line up so that our so-called life can begin—*and we will miss it!* While we are busy making plans, life can pass us by. This is a point well made in *Mr. Holland's Opus*, a 1995 movie about a musician with a desire to write one piece of music of lasting significance in order to leave his mark on the world. Glen Holland, the main character, goes to work on his composition, but employment as a pianist in a cocktail lounge does not take care of his financial obligations. Does he put life on hold because certain resources haven't come his way? No, he takes a job as a high school music teacher, and it turns into thirty years of his life—a time when he is able to invest in the lives of thousands of students, sharing his passion for music.

But Holland's much-dreamed-of orchestral composition is seemingly forever delayed. At the age of sixty, when his working life has come to an end, he believes it is too late to have his dream ever come true.

On his final day as a teacher, the despairing Mr. Holland is led to the school auditorium, where his professional life is surprisingly redeemed. Hearing that their beloved teacher is leaving, hundreds of his pupils have secretly returned to the school to celebrate his life.

> Mr. Holland's orchestral piece, never before heard in public, has been put before the musicians by his wife and son. One of the most musically challenged students, Gertrude Lang...who has become governor of the state, sits in with her clarinet. Gertrude and the other alumni ask the retiring teacher to serve as their conductor for the premiere performance of "Mr. Holland's Opus"...[2]

Glen Holland's legacy turned out to be greater than he had ever imagined. If he had never embraced what he needed to do and what was available for him to work with where he was at the time, he would have been left sitting, waiting for a break—and life would have passed him by. He would have never impacted the thousands of lives that he did, and he would have never had that moment that day in that high school auditorium, realizing that it was his very life that had turned into the memorable production that would transcend his time here on Earth and indeed leave a mark on this world. Yes, we can get so caught up in making plans and waiting for what we *think* we need to move forward with those plans—and life can go on without us, that is, without becoming all that it could have been.

A hindrance to many moving ahead is that they are waiting for what they think they need, not realizing that what they think they need is not always what they actually need, not at that time, not yet, and maybe never. Sometimes we are so busy looking for the big things, that we miss the little things that translate into big things in our lives. Paul tells us in 1 Corinthians 1:27–28 that God Himself uses foolish, weak, lowly, insignificant, and even things that are looked upon as contemptible, and even things that are considered nothing.

Is God telling us to settle for the mediocre and even less in life? Is He telling us not to work toward excellence in our lives and ministries? I don't think so. Paul gives us some insight when he says that "the foolishness of God is wiser than man's wisdom, and the weakness of God is stronger than man's strength" (1 Cor. 1:25). He tells us that God uses the "foolish to put the wise to shame, and what the world calls weak to put the strong to shame" (v. 27, AMP). In a nutshell, I believe we must take care in drawing our conclusions as to what is big and what is little, what is wise and what is foolish, what is strong and what is weak. Big things come in little packages—isn't that something that most of us have heard practically all our lives? I believe there is a lot of truth in this.

Even in Proverbs 30:24–28 we read (emphasis added):

> Four things on earth are small, yet they are extremely wise: Ants are creatures of little strength, yet they store up their food in the summer; coneys [rock badgers] are creatures of little power, yet they make their home in the crags; locusts have no king, yet they advance together in ranks; a lizard can be caught with the hand, yet it is found in kings' palaces.

The Bible has numerous examples of where God chose small things over big things. What about David? He was the youngest of eight brothers, only a boy, armed with a sling and five stones and no armor, spear, or sword, but he was used to defeat Goliath—the approximately nine-and-one-half-feet-tall Philistine giant, armed with helmet, coat of scale armor, a sword, and a spear, the head of which weighed about fifteen pounds? (See 1 Samuel 17.)

What about Gideon? His clan was "the weakest in Manasseh, and I am the least in my family" (Judg. 6:15), yet he was chosen to lead an army of three hundred against the armies of the Midianites, Amalekites, and other eastern peoples, thousands strong, "settled in the valley, thick as locust. Their camels could no more be counted than the sand of the seashore" (Judg. 7:12)?

What about *one* of God's prophets, Elijah, who was used in a showdown with 450 prophets of Baal and the 400 prophets of Asherah? (See 1 Kings 18:19.)

Speaking of God using the foolish things to confound the wise, think about how wise, how logical it seemed to leave ninety-nine sheep and go after the one that was lost. (See Luke 15:3–7.) Human reasoning would conclude that risking losing the other ninety-nine sheep while going after that one would not be the smartest move to make. But isn't it funny how a move like that makes a lot of sense when *you're* the one lost sheep.

It can become quite easy to get the impression that big is best. We can even become worshipers of "big," not understanding that what seems little, with Jesus in it, can become *very* big. We can become worshipers of winning and being first, forgetting that what looks like losing can be a great victory in disguise—like the crucifixion of Jesus, where a crown of thorns was turned into a crown of glory and what looked like the greatest defeat ever was the greatest victory ever to be won. And consider here Jesus' words about dying to live, or the last being first, or giving to receive.

We too often are either stunting or bringing to a complete halt our progress in life because we think we are too young, like Jeremiah, who, when God called him to speak to the nation of Judah, said in response to God, "Ah…I do not know how to speak; I am only a child" (Jer. 1:6). Or we think we are too old. What about Abraham, who when he was about a hundred years old and his wife's womb, in the natural, was dead, trusted God and believed for a son? (See Romans 4:19.)

And we can be stunting or completely halting our progress because we think we don't have enough or even anything at all that we really need to move forward. And here I repeat: we need to start with what we have and not necessarily what we think we need. What we have may not be what we want. It may not be what we desire, but it is what we need—at least, for the moment. But there are those who will groan and moan, "I didn't want this; I wanted that." And then they wonder why they produce children who are always complaining, "But, I wanted that!"

Along this line, we can make the mistake of attaching ourselves to certain wants or desires to the point of thinking we can't be happy without these, that we can't even make it without these. And we can pass this way of looking at life and reacting to life down to our children. Now, the wants and desires that I am talking about here are more so things—as in, more money or more stuff or certain kinds of stuff—that we think are necessary for us to be happy, and that if we don't have these things, we flat out refuse to be happy and even go forward with our lives. We must not confuse the acquiring of things with being happy and prosperous. Sometimes it is not so much letting go of a desire or dream but of a wrong attachment to it.

We need to take what we have and use it. I've found out time and time again that when you think you are at the end of your rope, there is always a way. I've found out that when you get to a place where you've seemingly run out of options and seemingly run out of resources that is when your eyes can be opened to something you've been missing right under your nose. It was there all the time—just like Jesus is.

Jesus took two fish and five loaves and turned them into a meal for five thousand men, plus the women and the children—and still had twelve baskets of leftovers. (See Matthew 14:17–21.) We need to pray to have our eyes opened to see what God has put around us and within us *already*, to be able to recognize these things; and then we need to start from there.

Some haven't received more yet because they haven't used what they have. I think the message that Jesus was trying to get across in Luke 16:10–12 was along this line. He said that if we can be trusted with very little, we can be trusted with much; that if we can be trusted with worldly wealth, we can be trusted with true riches; and that if we can be trusted with someone else's property, we can be given our own property. It just makes good sense to not give someone more if he or she has made no effort to use what is already in hand. And people have all kinds of things at their fingertips that they don't use. They are wanting something else, and they don't use what they already have. So, they sit around and whine: whine, whine, whine, bellyaching and complaining that "I'm not smart. I don't read or write well. I don't have this and I can't do that." You might not have certain talents, a lot of certain talents, but you do have talent. It is somewhere in you. You might not be able to do certain things, a lot of certain things, but there is something that you can do, and can do well. And you can even learn to do it better.

Stop whining about what you don't have or what you can't do and start using what you have and doing what you can—and to the best of your ability. It's the whining that will stop you, not what you don't have. It's the whining that kept the children of Israel from going on into the Promised Land. They got tired of the manna, so God rained down quail. And then they got tired of that. A whining spirit is never satisfied, like the four things mentioned in Proverbs 30:15–16 that never say, "Enough!"—the grave, the barren womb, the earth that is not filled with water, and fire.

If one thing doesn't work, use another. There is success story after success story about individuals who were diminished in one area, even totally deprived in that area—such as a body part or faculty or a talent or a resource of some kind or other—and they went on to accomplish great feats, using another body part or faculty or a talent or a resource that they *did* have. Joni Eareckson Tada, for example, after a diving accident that left her paralyzed from the neck down, went on to paint masterpieces with a paintbrush between her teeth. How does our excuse for not moving forward compare to Joni's?

I repeat: If one thing doesn't work, use another. And we must stop envying someone else and coveting what he or she has. And we don't want to miss our blessing if just maybe God has us helping someone else to use more effectively what that person has or better do what that person can do—you know, like when Jesus was saying that if we can be trusted with someone else's property, we can be given our own property. (See Luke 16:12.) And it's not that you help others to be successful so you can be given something yourself. Helping others to be successful is its own reward—at least, it will be for the person who knows what it is to *truly* live.

There are those who want nothing to do with helping others to be better positioned for success in their lives. For them, it's got to be all about *me! Me! Me!* It becomes about doing for *me.* It becomes about being sure that *I'm* the one who gets to reap the benefits (though I said that helping others to be successful is its own reward—is a benefit). It becomes about being sure that *I'm* the one who gets the recognition, the applause, the notoriety. It becomes about working for *my* ministry, building *my* ministry. In becoming lone rangers and disconnecting from others (unless they can help *me*), the individual short-sheets himself.

I think Paul has something to contribute to this discussion when in Romans 8:28 he says, "And we know that in all things God works for the good of those who love him, who have been called according to his purpose." Some people are not experiencing all things being worked for their good because they are not walking in God's purpose for their lives. God's purpose, perhaps only for a certain season, may be for you to be helping someone else, though being willing to help others when and where it is called for should always be a part of our make-up. After all, we will never exist in this world—and especially as a part of the body of Christ—as an island. We may try, but it won't work. We are one of many members; we are a part of a whole. We are connected. We need each other. We must work together. And this means that "if one part is honored, every part rejoices with it" (1 Cor. 12:26). So using what I have and doing what I can *now* mean sticking with God's purpose for me for this season of my life.

I've been talking about getting rid of the victim mentality in our lives. I remember feeling sorry for myself for a long time over a span of many, many years following the suicide attempts, and then the divorce and car accidents, and then the rape and abortion and disease (that I will discuss in chapters to come). *Poor little Valinda! Woe is me! Woe is me! Woe is me!* But the day came when the Lord brought me out of this, and it is no longer, *Woe is me!*

For the biggest part of my life it was, *Poor little Valinda; she doesn't have a mother! Poor little Valinda!* But the many truths that I have discovered along the way—which I share in the pages of this volume—set me free. Actually, it was *the* truth that set me free. (See John 8:32.) I truly came to find out that "if God is for us [and oh, how very much He is], who can be against us?" (Rom. 8:31).

PART V

MIRACLE POTTERY

Chapter 16

CLOSED HEAD INJURY

M ANY TIMES I have been asked how I came to make pottery. And my answer is always, "Huh! It's a *miracle* that I can make pottery. Let me tell you the story."

And people seem to always be amazed at how this came about—for one reason, because I don't have any extensive *or* professional training in this craft, such as a degree in pottery or ceramic arts. But a second reason why people are amazed is that I had a tremendous handicap that absolutely disqualified me from ever being what I have become today—not only in the pottery-making business but in life, *period*. It was God who miraculously qualified and enabled me to make pottery.

Prior to becoming a pottery maker, I had owned several businesses, such as restaurants and a grocery store. At one time I owned three restaurants, an old-timey grocery store, and an old-timey meat market. And prior to that I was a real estate agent. I've been a dental assistant, a chiropractic therapist, and an X-ray technician. I've done a number of things in my life.

The day came when my husband and I sold all of the businesses and decided that we would retire. And I had to laugh at that because I had tried to retire several times, but I just didn't know how to quit working. Having been a single parent and sole supporter of my children for *many, many* years, taking on as many as four jobs at a time, I just wasn't geared to know what to do with myself if I was not working all the time.

Therefore, I decided to go back to work after we sold the businesses. Desiring a good retirement plan, I took on employment at a major, multi-billion-dollar corporation and worked my way up from sales to upper management. I was doing quite well and enjoying my high-powered life in the corporate world, traveling over the Southeast with a company car and an expense account. But then a near-fatal automobile accident changed all of that.

The vehicle I was driving was rear-ended by another car, pushing my vehicle to a bluff's edge. I regained consciousness with no time to spare. It was a split-second thing; *something* caused me to immediately apply my foot to the brake. I know it was God. Otherwise, I should have spiraled down that cliff's steep face to a blazing, crumpled, and gnarled metal grave.

In the course of this tragedy, my seatbelt caught me across the neck and cut off my air supply. That's why I don't like to wear seatbelts to this day, though I do. I couldn't breathe and believe that this cutting off of my air supply contributed to the head injury I suffered as a result.

But the primary cause of my head injury had to do with what can happen to one's brain when his or her vehicle is rear-ended. When a car is struck from behind, the brain inside the skull of the rear-ended vehicle's passenger is thrust forward. Having a consistency comparable to a bowl of Jell-O, the frontal lobes—the front part of each hemisphere or half of the brain—slap against the skull. And then the brain is propelled backward. And then the brain is propelled forward and backward again and again—with the duration of that depending on the force of the vehicle's collision. Finally the brain settles down, but the back-and-forth movement leaves it bruised. Every time it impacted the skull it was bruised.

In my case, the driver of the rear-ending vehicle never applied his brakes, while I was at a dead stop when he slammed into me. I was at a dead stop in the road because the car in front of me had come to a sudden stop and then immediately whipped into a gas station. I managed to stop in time not to rear-end that vehicle, but the car that came over the hill behind me did not fare as well and rammed me without so much as tapping his brakes.

In lieu of this, I was fortunate that the traumatic brain injury I suffered was a closed (rather than open) head injury, so my skull and the outermost covering of the brain remained intact.[1] I was blessed, as well, that the closed head injury I suffered resulted only in short-term memory loss (though the repercussions of that were near-devastating to me), since closed head injuries have the potential of inflicting *life-long* physical, cognitive (perception, memory, judgment, and reasoning), or psychological impairment. I totally and absolutely thank God that the brain damage was not so severe as to result in a coma or vegetative state, even death—which were all possibilities.[2]

I experienced all the common symptoms of a closed head injury—headache, dizziness, nausea, slurred speech, and vomiting.[3] The headaches were so severe as to nearly incapacitate me for weeks and weeks at a time. Not able to hold my head up and not thinking I could live, I was left to lie on the sofa on most days, as there were few good days in any month.

Patients recovering from a closed head or traumatic brain injury often suffer from decreased self-esteem as well. In looking back on my personal experience in this regard, I find this to be quite the understatement in light of the feelings of worthlessness, depression, and social anxiety that were mine to bear as I traveled the road to rehabilitation and regaining of cognitive skills that a closed head injury can impair.

My situation was that I still had memory of all the things that I had been able to do prior to the accident, and I'd think I could still do them, but I couldn't connect the dots. If I got into the car to drive, I couldn't remember to turn left or right. I might be out driving and end up three states away, especially since I lived in a geographical area where the converging of states was such that this could happen before a tank of gas had run out, and then, feeling so lost, I would go into a full-blown panic attack. I'd sometimes be found passed out on the side of the road somewhere.

I would be in a state of panic because I couldn't remember where I had been or where I was going, and, therefore, couldn't even ask for directions. And I couldn't ask for directions to get back to my home because I couldn't remember what road I was supposed to be on to get back home.

If I did manage to find a phone booth—there weren't cell phones back then—there often wasn't anyone around for me to ask, "Where is this town? What road am I on?" And you don't want to be asking a rank stranger, "Where is this place? What town or state am I in?" So I panicked, but I could at least call home if I managed to override the panic and get to a phone. I could then call home, because my phone number was in my old memory bank. But then I didn't know where I was to tell my husband or children or a friend where to come get me.

My husband would ask, "Well, where are you?"

And I would answer, "Well, if I knew where I was, I wouldn't be lost."

And he'd say, "But, honey, you don't understand; I can't come get you if I don't know where you are." And he'd continue, "Just calm down and look around you and tell me what you see."

And after I looked around and told him what I saw—the motels or restaurants or whatever was around me—he would try to figure out what city or town or state I was in. He would tell me to look all around to see what I could see. And not having a cell phone, I couldn't keep traveling until I came upon something that might be significant or familiar to him. So, depending on what I saw from that phone booth or public place that had a phone I could use, my husband would try to figure out where I was—even the very state to which I had wandered.

Sometimes he would calculate where I was because he would figure that I had taken some route that I had taken many years prior. And he would then say, "Just go get a motel room; get that motel room across the way. Get a room there, and I'll come get you."

And I could be as much as four hours away from him. I could have driven that far and that long without realizing it, failing to connect the dots of time and distance. And the day my car keys were taken from me, they might as well have shot me, because those keys and that car represented my independence. They were connected to my self-esteem.

I couldn't watch TV, because I didn't have the power of concentration that was needed. If a commercial came on, I was lost when whatever I was watching resumed. I couldn't read, because by the time I got to the end of the sentence—even one little sentence—I had forgotten the beginning of the sentence, the first word. I had crocheted and knitted before, but now I couldn't keep track of how many stitches I had done, so I couldn't crochet or knit anymore.

To me, for all practical purposes, I couldn't do anything—not anything. I couldn't cook, and here I had owned and managed and cooked in restaurants in times past. If I had a skillet of grease on the stove, I might end up going outside, forgetting all about what I was cooking or that I was cooking *period*, and the house would be on fire. I'd be getting ready to take a bath and forget that I had turned the water on to fill the tub, and the tub would end up overflowing; water would be flooding the place. I'd be back in the bedroom somewhere, oblivious that I had been getting my water ready for a bath.

I just did all kinds of crazy things, just like an Alzheimer's patient would do. I'd think I could do something and would go try, but then I would lose my train of thought and end up somewhere else doing something else. So I had to have a 24-7 keeper—might as well call it a babysitter—to keep me out of trouble, to keep me from burning the house down, to keep me from running water out into the floor, to keep me from being lost.

Here I was—somebody who had worked three and four jobs at a time, owned several businesses, and had been in the corporate world, having a number of people working under me. And now all I seemingly was capable of doing was watching the fish swim in the aquarium. And I did have some of the most precious little fish in the world; they were chocolate-colored lionhead orandas with wide, massive heads compared to other goldfish and with faces that looked like fish versions of bulldogs. They were like miniature puppies to me; I had actually trained them to swim up into my hand and allow me to pet them. They would take turns doing this.

There were two of them. I had them for years and absolutely loved them. And now the only thing I seemed to be able to do with my life was sit there and watch my fish swim in their aquarium, which was a fifty-five-gallon tank. I did manage to clean the tank; I kept somewhat busy managing to do that much. But then I would forget that I had just fed my lionheads, so I would feed them and feed them and feed them—until I killed my fish. I was devastated because I loved my fish and had fed them to death. I killed them because I overfed them.

And, then, what was left for me? I couldn't watch TV. I couldn't cook. I couldn't drive. I couldn't even take good care of myself. I just wanted to die every day. And I'd pray, "God just please let me die; don't leave me in this body like this." I had all the knowledge of owning and operating restaurants, of doing real estate transactions, of being a therapist, a dental assistant, and an X-ray technician, and had used my brain for marketing and sales; and now, in a moment's time, I no longer could depend on my brain.

I had all this knowledge and memory of how to do these things, but with my short-term memory impaired, all this knowledge was virtually useless. I couldn't take advantage of it; I couldn't operate in it. As far as I was concerned, as far as what had made my life count for something, I could do nothing, nothing, nothing! I had to have a keeper, and everybody would get so frustrated with me because all I could do was make messes of anything I tried to do everywhere I went.

There was even talk of admitting me to an institution. The doctor said that it probably would be best if I was put in an institution—that I would never, ever be any better, that I would just continue to get worse. And when that devastating prognosis was delivered to me, more than ever I no longer wanted to keep on living. What did I have to live for? There are some things that are worse than death, and to be left shut up in a body like the one I was in was one of those things.

Whenever I see Alzheimer's patients today, my heart breaks. And it does, as well, for these young men and women coming back from war that are in the same shape that I was in—suffering from a closed-head brain injury. One day my pottery shop will help rehabilitate girls and guys like that, just like making pottery, as I am going to share, was used to rehabilitate me. I am working even now to get grants for a large enough facility in which I can teach both those with closed head injuries and young children who have autism to be able to do something with their hands that their body doesn't want to do, to bring meaningful life back to something that doesn't work anymore. That is my dream. And one day it will happen because the Lord has told me as much.

He has even shown me the facility. I have a picture of it hanging on the wall, and it will become a reality. I have the land, and I'm working on getting the grants for the facility itself. I even know the exact location, the exact spot where that building will stand and where the parking lot will be and how the landscape will look—*I've seen it all.*

And I know exactly how to operate this undertaking. I've even talked to schools that can and desperately want to get grants to enroll their autistic children in this program. Handicapped children can be tremendously benefited by the activities that will be offered. Soldiers caught in exploding tanks and left with all their old memory but no longer having their short-term memory intact—I will be able to help them.

But getting back to my story, there was talk of putting me in an institution. As an entrepreneur, and a pretty successful one at that, I had so depended on my brain. You know, you can't get a real estate license if you're a dummy. And, now, all of a sudden, my short-term memory was impaired, and I could no longer count on my brain like I had before. What was I to do? Where was I to go?

Chapter 17

POTTERY THERAPY

A DEAR FRIEND, A counselor at a local high school, came by to see me, and she suggested that I try art as therapy. She said, "Valinda, sometimes you can use the artistic side of your brain." She told me which side that was. I didn't realize that there was an artistic side of the brain. And then she, in essence, said that if the side of your brain that has to do with short-term memory is not working up to snuff, you can use the other side of your brain, and it will sometimes trigger your memory.

And I said to my friend, "That's a lovely thought, and it just sounds beautiful. But I don't have any artistic ability. I can't draw a stick man."

And she rebounded, stating, "Well, Valinda, *everybody* has talent; it can just be hidden."

And I said, "Well, yes, then mine's hidden *real* good; it's still out under a big rock somewhere, because it's never come forth."

"Well, I'm going to go take a pottery class," she continued, "and I want you to go with me. And I'll drive you because I know you can't drive anymore."

And I questioned, "Pottery class?"

She answered, "Yes."

And I asked, "Isn't that with clay, like you put on a wheel and that kind of thing?"

I knew absolutely *nothing* about pottery other than what I had just stated. Oh, I knew that when I saw pottery, I thought it was beautiful, but that's about all I knew about the matter. Then I recollected, "Well, come to think of it, when I was a kid, I used to make my little wares and arrange them around the edge of the mud puddle. A little bird nest and little plates and saucers and things—I'd place them around the mud puddle's edge. And mother used to spank me for messing up my clothes."

On second thought, I decided, "You know, that does sound like fun; I'd like that. I'd like to go to that pottery class."

And so my friend and I attended a class about pottery, taught by a local teacher. I don't remember now if it was a one-week or two-week class, but I do remember working with the kick wheel, the kind of pottery wheel that is manpowered, or woman-powered in my case. It's a big, round wheel, heavy-leaded on the bottom, and you just kick it with your foot, causing the smaller wheel at the top to go around. You kick it one way with one foot and then back the other way with the other foot. And it keeps going around and around. I have one in my own shop today.

But I also have an electric wheel; I have several electric wheels. But the kick wheel is what I started out on. And, as it was, the teacher of that pottery class was not impressed with me. She simply did not think I had the necessary skill or was hopeful that I could even acquire the necessary skill to make beautiful pottery. But she probably was the very best teacher that I could have had, because I'm not the kind of person that has "give up" in me. I'm not discouraged very easily.

There is an odd but quite interesting statement that has been made: friends will give you comfort, but enemies will bring increase or promotion. That is to say that without a Goliath, you are going to be feeding sheep the rest of your life when there is something else on the horizon for you. It has been said of David when he saw the Philistine giant, Goliath, that he didn't say, "Oh, my God, he is too big *to hit*," but rather, "Oh, my God, he is too big *to miss*." And it was not David's stone but actually the giant's own sword that was used by David to bring about the giant's demise. What seems to be the very thing that the enemy uses against you to fuel and empower his onslaught—as in discouraging words, put-downs, ridicule—can be the very thing that will fuel and empower your increase or promotion.

That particular pottery teacher was probably the best teacher that I could have had because she just pretty much said that I couldn't do the job—that I wasn't going to make a potter *at all*, that I just wasn't going to make it... *period*.

I bristled and stood up on the inside to say, *Wow, I'll show her!*

That lady discouraged me from the very beginning. But she just didn't know what that one little pot in her class meant to me, as pitiful as it might have looked after I got through crafting it, because that pot to me was my first accomplishment in about four years—*my first accomplishment!* Yes, it had been about four years since the accident, and every day of those four years, I wanted to die. But finally I had my first accomplishment, and that teacher, whether consciously or not, was trying to take that away from me.

She had no idea what that pitiful little pot meant to me. And I still have that pot—I wouldn't take anything for it, because making it was life changing for me. I saw myself as having been reduced to that piece of clay. And as God allowed me to mold that little bowl in that class, it was as if He were molding me and giving me a new purpose in life, a reason to live again. And that, at that time, meant *everything* to me; it meant *life* to me.

I was thinking, *If I can make this one pot, I can make another one, and another one, and another one. This is an accomplishment.*

When I no longer could depend on my memory—my short-term memory in particular—where could I go? What did I have left? I looked at my hands, and they still worked. God had not left me without a way. In looking back on life, He never had; He had never left me without a way. I give Him credit for something I believe He instilled in me a long time ago, as having been created in His image—He is not a quitter, *and neither am I.*

With no education and two children, I got a job. And if one paycheck wasn't enough, I got two jobs and then three and then four. It wasn't easy, but it paid off. I had learned not to stop and say, "If somebody doesn't help me, I can't make it." More often than not, there was nobody else. My mother died. My husband walked away. My dad refused.

That was what I had come to know for starters: Be happy with what you have, and don't whine about it. Don't dwell on what you don't have. If you find that something doesn't work anymore, then shift gears. If you don't have all your mental faculties, use your hands. If you don't have your hands, use your feet. If the right hand doesn't work, use the left one. If the left foot doesn't work, use the right one. God is waiting to give us something else when we are grateful for and use what we have. He will *always* make a way.

I could have allowed that teacher to rob me of my destiny, but I didn't. She spent *minimal* time teaching me how to glaze and fire my creation, and I believe it was because she saw no potential in me. The class was designed to take the students through the whole process of pottery-making; but when it came to me, my teacher did not see the investment as worthwhile. So, actually, she fired my pot while I wasn't there, denying me the experience of doing it myself. I picked my pot up later. But I was still so intrigued by this craft and the art it produced.

I had lost so much due to the car accident that resulted in my head injury. Needless to say, I lost my job. Charges were drummed up to make a way for me to be fired because I was not useful to the company anymore. And, of course, my company car went out the door with my employment.

Not having a job meant I did not have the finances I once had, and I needed finances because I now wanted to buy a kick wheel for making pottery on my own. Unable to buy one, I hired somebody to make me a kick wheel, to build one for me. I then bought an old, used kiln. That's what you use to fire the pottery.

I bought myself a little book that taught me the steps to making pottery. And I added that knowledge to what I had acquired in those few pottery classes I had taken. And then I called the supply house where I could purchase my clay for making pottery, and I asked their representative about the kiln I had bought. I didn't even know what cones were, and I didn't know what a cone-setter was—with the cone being a triangular piece of material that indicates by bending or melting that a certain temperature has been reached. I didn't know what kind of "furniture" was needed.

Personnel at that supply house, via long distance, taught me how to glaze and fire my pottery—how to mix glazes and how to fire. I hadn't been aware that you almost have to be a chemist to mix glazes—to mix all those chemicals to come up with various colors.

The supply house people were kind and helpful, and other individuals were as well. There were potters who shared their pottery recipes, and you follow those recipes like following a recipe for baking a cake. You buy the chemicals and mix your glazes a certain way according to the recipe, and they come out the way you want—and in some of the richest and most vibrant colors you can imagine.

So I sat on my porch on Lookout Mountain overlooking a lake, and I started making pots. I crafted pottery using an old-fashioned kick wheel, and it brought *great* satisfaction. The mental acuity involved in crafting pottery is a considerably few notches above that required for putting a pan of grease on the stove to fry chicken. Something was kicking in for me. I was operating a pottery wheel, mixing chemicals, and working with a high-temperature kiln. Little by little, day after day, month after month, sitting at that wheel—just me and that piece of clay and that potter's wheel and nobody else around—this connecting was going on in my brain. One side of my brain was being used to cause the other side to kick in. It was like building a muscle; it was a slow process, so slow that I didn't even realize the change that was taking place in my mental processes.

I was taking a necessary step to getting somewhere. Some people want to arrive overnight at their goal and are not willing to take the necessary steps to getting there. If we will just keep the goal in sight, the road will not seem near as difficult and long, and in the end, the journey will not have been such a high price to pay. In some ways, I believe the journey itself can turn out to be even more, or, at least, just as valuable as the ultimate goal itself. Remember *Mr. Holland's Opus*?

Chapter 18

STRONG CONNECTION BETWEEN POTTERY AND PEOPLE

I HAD STARTED CRAFTING pottery. And it is significant to my story that there is a strong connection between pottery and people. God Himself makes use of this analogous relationship more than once in Scripture when He refers to Himself as being the Potter and to us as being the clay:

> Yet, O Lord, you are our Father. We are the clay, you are the potter; we are all the work of your hand.
>
> —ISAIAH 64:8

> So I went down to the potter's house, and I saw him working at the wheel. But the pot he was shaping from the clay was marred in his hands; so the potter formed it into another pot, shaping it as seemed best to him. the word of the Lord came to me: "O house of Israel, can I not do with you as this potter does?" declares the Lord. "Like clay in the hand of the potter, so are you in my hand, O house of Israel.
>
> —JEREMIAH 18:3–6

Pottery can be classified into three main categories—earthenware, stoneware, and porcelain. In making a point, let's take porcelain, for example. This ceramic material is celebrated for its qualities of purity of color, the permitting of light to pass through its walls, its strength, and that when fired to the right high temperature, it will "ring" if tapped. If we apply this to human beings, oh, how desirable these qualities are in us, as well. But porcelain, compared to other categories of ceramic art, has to be fired at significantly higher temperatures.

And, in addition to that, porcelain is the least plastic of the ceramic materials, meaning that it is the least capable of being molded or receiving form. It is quite challenging to "control and manipulate on the wheel." And one way to increase this material's plasticity is "to let it 'age' for as long as possible between the time it is mixed wet and the time it is thrown [or shaped, as on the potter's wheel]."[1] Does that not ring a bell when we think about how God sometimes has to let us "age" between the time we think we are all "mixed" and ready to see things take place and the time when things actually take shape? He has to increase our "plasticity" and deal with our resistance to being shaped and molded the way we need to be.

And then porcelain is referred to as "the aristocrat of the potter's art." Yet, a high percentage of the recognized masterpieces of the ceramic arts are of earthenware and stoneware.[2] This makes me think of what Paul said about the body of Christ in 1 Corinthians 14:

> Now the body is not made up of one part but of many....If the whole body were an eye, where would the sense of hearing be? If the whole body were an ear, where would the sense of smell be?... The eye cannot say to the hand, "I don't need you!" And the head cannot say to the feet, "I don't need you!" On the contrary, those parts of the body that seem to be weaker are indispensable, and the parts that we think are less honorable we treat with special honor.
>
> —1 CORINTHIANS 12:14, 17, 21–23

With pottery classified into three main categories—earthenware, stoneware, and porcelain—the means to the desired end are infinitely variable. And these means depend primarily upon the intended purpose of the pottery and the certain combination called for of such criteria as forming technique, firing technique, and chemistry of clay and glaze.[3] Likewise, God's means in the crafting of our destinies are variable. His methods and resources are unlimited. We are not stuck—unless we settle for that. God knows our purpose, our future, our destiny—and He knows what is needed to see it all come to pass.

Three main ways that clay may be formed are using the potter's wheel, handbuilding, and using molds (a process called "slip-casting"). The potter's wheel allows for rapid stretching and shaping of the clay. Hand-building, which predates the use of the potter's wheel, involves "pinching, coiling, working with slabs, as well as carving clay."[4] And when it comes to creating "identical forms" and large numbers of product—what manufacturing is all about—slip-casting is the way to go. Remember, slip-casting uses molds, with the mold guaranteeing that all the pieces will conform to the same shape and size—you know, the cookie-cutter approach.

It is pointed out that "in our technologically oriented and cost-effective world, handmade pottery isn't necessary."[5] I am of the opinion and so is Scripture that when it comes to the fashioning of our lives, God throws costeffectiveness to the wind and spares no expense on our behalf—even to the very death of His Son for us on Calvary. I am of the opinion that God finds the handmade method quite necessary in the forming and shaping of the clay peculiar to each one of us. He was at work doing this while we were still in our mother's womb—"For you created my inmost being; you knit me together in my mother's womb" (Ps. 139:13).

And when it comes to the forming of clay by the method of slip-casting, I am convinced that God doesn't use molds, and therefore, He doesn't use the slip-casting method at all—*not at all*. We are each unique and special. No one else is like us, and no one can take our place. And for this very reason, as an artist, I like to create each piece of my pottery differently, like snowflakes, where there are no two alike. No two pieces of my pottery are exactly alike, whether they are bowls or platters or cups. At Miracle Pottery, we don't make anything with a mold. Everything is made by hand, with the assistance sometimes of a potter's wheel—but custom-designed, just like God does with us.

Every one of God's created beings is different. Our individual bent, including our personality, is different from that of others. Our talents are different. And I like to go as far as to say that it's OK to be different. I deliberately dress differently; I make it a point to have things that nobody else has anything like. I don't try to dress according to the latest trend, because I choose to be different because God created me that way. He didn't create me from a mold. If He had, I believe He would have thrown the mold away in order to not make another one just like me.

God made each one of us individually, and we must beware of trying to fit into some kind of mold. We must beware of going along in life trying to be like so-and-so.

We say, "Well, so-and-so did it this way; and it worked," or, "So-and-so did it that way, and it worked." And then we try to do the same thing, and it may not be what God has called us to do. God called us to do what He called *us* to do—not what so-and-so is doing. We're not made with a cookie-cutter.

"But, it worked for so-and-so," we say.

But it might not work for us—not if we're not called to do it. Something can be a good idea and of itself be perfectly OK, but it's not OK if God hasn't called us to do it. And something else might seem off-the-wall, but it's right on if that's what God has called us to do. That off-the-wall thing might be carrying out a ministry in a pottery shop—as opposed to doing so in a church. But that's OK if that's where God has you, if that's what He wants you doing. And today I'm happy—doing what He called me to do!

I'm still talking about the strong connection between pottery and people. It is the firing process in the making of pottery that converts what could be very fragile material into something durable and strong. Now that sounds like something I've read before: "The refining pot is for silver and the furnace for gold" (Prov. 17:3, AMP). It's when the gold is put in the furnace that all the impurities are brought forth. Impurities can compromise the strength of a substance. And the Bible compares this to people who, under fire, have the impurities in their heart brought to the surface. When things that are impure are exposed, they can then be dealt with. Impurities can be hidden, but fire will bring them to the surface. The temperature required in the firing process in making pottery has to do with the *purpose* of the pottery. Earthenware calls for kiln temperatures below 1200 degrees Celsius (or 2055 degrees Fahrenheit), while stoneware is fired at temperatures between 1200 and 1300 degrees C (or 2201 and 2381 degrees F). Porcelain, on the other hand, is the result of firing at 1300 degrees C (or 2610 degrees F) or more.[6]

Yet another analogy can be drawn between pottery and people—with purpose connected to the degree and kind of preparedness that is required. It is noteworthy that the more yielded the clay is to being shaped and to retaining that shape once it dries, the stronger it will be in the firing process.[7] This makes me think of how yielded the three Hebrews Shadrach, Meshach, and Abednego were to their God and how strong they were when they were cast into King Nebuchadnezzar's blazing furnace of fire. The end result was that "the fire had not harmed their bodies, nor was a hair of their heads singed; their robes were not scorched, and there was no smell of fire on them" (Dan. 3:27). All that was burned were the ropes that bound them.

This property of clay yielding itself to being shaped—called plasticity—allows for it to be:

> Pulled up into high thin-walled forms without tearing or subsequent slumping. It allows a shape once formed to be radically modified or indeed totally altered without collapse or disintegration and, further, it allows satellite forms such as handles, spouts or high relief decoration to be wielded on to the parent mass and to retain this positive adhesion as the clay stiffens and dries.[8]

Now, if we would think about it, this says a lot about the possibilities *we* have of being stretched or "pulled" beyond our limits to be and do and have more, of being "radically modified or indeed totally altered without collapse or disintegration" when necessary and even desired, and of having things added or "wielded" to us that we presently don't have but could enhance us in some needed or desired way—if we will yield to our Father, if we will be "plastic" in His hands, if we will "commit [our] way to the Lord; trust in him" (Ps. 37:5). If we will, He promises to bring His purposes for our lives to pass. How very sensible it is to look to and be pliable in the hands of the one who knows the end from the beginning, who has our best interests at heart, and with whom nothing is impossible!

Categories of pottery, forming techniques, the firing technique, including the degree of yieldedness or plasticity of the ceramic material—these all have something to say about the Master Potter molding us, the clay. And continuing to show the strong connection between pottery and people, there is yet another comparison to be seen when it comes to *centering* the clay on the potter's wheel. This must take place first, before the shaping can begin.

It takes total concentration to center a piece of clay from which you intend to fashion an object of pottery. The hands must be absolutely still as that clay goes around and around with your hands guiding it and defining its parameters. And when the clay is no longer wobbling around, you know that it's centered. It is then that the potter commences to stretch the clay up into space and then shape it into a pleasing form. You can't do anything with that piece of clay until you get it centered.

And God can't *truly* shape us into that beautiful object of art that we were intended to be until He gets us centered in His will. He created each of us with a purpose in mind, and when our desire is to be in the center of God's will, as in fulfilling His purpose for our lives, then the stretching and shaping can transpire with so much more ease and at a much quicker pace. He knows how to smooth out all the rough places.

And if we are wobbling around—"like a wave of the sea, blown and tossed by the wind....double-minded...unstable" (James 1:6, 8)—that's a good sign that we are not centered in God's will. We've lost our single-mindedness, our focus on and trust in Him. James 1:7 says, "That man should not think he will receive anything from the Lord." Good things can destroy us if we are not at a place of maturity to handle them or when we are at a place where we might misuse or abuse them. God doesn't withhold good things from us to be mean; it's just that wobbling clay is not ready for the shaping and molding and even wielding of the extras (handles, spouts, or high relief decoration) that could enhance the pot that it could be. Very similarly to how clay is shaped into a vessel of usefulness and beauty, God is forming us.

And one last point I will make about the similarity between pottery and people has to do with the similarity between God's crafting of *me* as a human being and *my* crafting of pottery. An accomplished artisan in ceramic arts describes "an intimate relationship" going on in the process of crafting pottery.[9] And that is indeed true of the crafting of human beings at the hands of the Potter of the ages.

Now, God hasn't merely crafted us; He is our creator. And even more, He has created us in His image. If we are created in the image of God, what does that mean? This implies *more* than what takes place when an artisan creates a painting or musical composition or sculpture. This implies that God's very image is engrained in us. So what do we know about this God in whose image we are created? What was He doing, as recorded in the Word, up to the time that He said, "Let us make man in our image, in our likeness" (Gen. 1:26)? *He was creating!* We are created in the likeness of one who creates. That tells me that inherent in our design and makeup is the desire and ability to create.

I didn't understand at the time, but making pottery is a way to release creative ability. I was stirring up and releasing my creative juices as I sat at that potter's wheel; I was pouring creative energy and ability into one lump of clay after another. And as I was molding that ceramic material into creations of art, God was molding me.

The clay that was my life had been reduced. The prophet Jeremiah said, "The clay was marred" (Jer. 18:4). I had been sharp and accomplished in the corporate world—wearing expensive suites, exquisite jewelry, snakeskin shoes, thinking I was somebody. But that had changed. I was broken, shattered, damaged. All my trappings had been removed, and now my Father could make something of real worth out of me—"so the potter formed it into another pot, shaping it as seemed best to him" (Jer. 18:4).

I find myself making a connection here with what Jesus said in Matthew 16:19 when He said that He has given us keys—"whatever you bind on earth will be bound in heaven, and whatever you loose on earth will be loosed in heaven." I believe that as I yielded my hands to pick up that clump of clay, I gave God something to work with. And once I did that, I triggered, I "loosed" creative energy and ability, allowing God to, in turn, loose in heaven on my behalf creative energy and ability that was restoring my mind.

My friend who came to my rescue spoke of how God has physically wired us so that if the side of our brain that has to do with short-term memory is not working up to snuff, we can use the other side of our brain, the artistic, or right, side, and it will sometimes trigger our memory. But I believe that a spiritual principle is involved here as well whereby we become our Father's hands, feet, eyes, etc.—even His voice—on this earth. We are the body of Christ! And He is waiting for us to release so that He can, in turn, release out of heaven on our behalf. He is waiting for us to bind, so He can do so out of heaven. We become laborers *together* with Him. We become co-creators with Him. That's being a family, and that's what He's about!

So I kept making those pots, day after day after day. And little by little, God was working on me, as well—on my memory.

Chapter 19

YOU REALLY WANT TO BUY THIS?

M Y HUSBAND CAME out to my work area one day and asked, "Valinda, what are you going to do with all these pots?"
And I said, "Well, I don't know. I hadn't thought about it. But I'm out of trouble. I'm not burning the house down. I'm not running water out in the floor. Just leave me be; I'm out of trouble."

I was staying out of the kitchen, as far as cooking went. My husband was taking care of that. I was pretty much staying out of the way period, except to go inside to get something to eat. I was content going into my little studio to work day after day after day. This went on for months, and those pots kept mounting up. And I kept getting better and better and better and better.

So my husband asked, "Valinda, what are you going to do with all these pots?"

I didn't rightly know, and I didn't want him to stop me from making them. I said, "I've got to keep making them!"

He said, "But you've got so many of them. You've got to recoup some of your money that you're spending out here. You might ought to try to sell some of them."

Sell them? It hadn't occurred to me to sell them. I was just thinking of staying out of trouble while trying to accomplish something with my life. I had been used to being an ambitious, adventurous, and career-driven person, and that seemingly had been taken from me. But now I was busy again. It was important that I stayed busy. So opening a shop across the street from the restaurant I once owned in Mentone, Alabama, allowed me to stay busy and sell my pottery at the same time. It was just a little bitty place that we fixed up, painted, and got to looking real spiffy, and I placed my pottery wares out to be sold.

We live in a little resort town that people come to from all over the country, literally from all over the world. And people started coming into my shop and buying my pots. And I remember holding them up and saying, "You *really* want to buy this?"

And they'd ask, "Well, is it for sale?"

Part of me was surprised that anyone would want to buy these articles that I had made. They were mere wads of clay that had been transformed by me and really weren't worth much—my teacher had made me feel that way, you know. And, on the other hand, I caught myself holding on to my pots and not wanting to let them go because they were so precious to me—they were special accomplishments that had come after a time in my life when I thought I would never be able to accomplish anything of significance again. So mixed emotions went into my asking, "You really want to buy this?"

But people kept buying my pots, and they would buy all I had. I was even supplying shops in Gatlinburg and New Orleans. And I thought, "Wow! I can't believe this!"

They just kept buying them. Encouraged by this, I'd go make some more pots. And the crowd would come the next weekend and buy them all again. I was thrilled.

Now the lady next door had a bigger shop, one where she sold these creations with heads and cute little bodies fashioned from gourds. And then she wrote a book explaining how these creations, called *gourdies*, came to be. Tourists loved these and came from all over the country to buy them.

One day this neighboring shop owner approached me with an offer: "Valinda, you don't have much room in your shop. Why don't you leave your kilns there and bring your wheel to my shop? Customers can watch you making your pots, and you can manage my shop for me while you're selling your product. With me living over here in Huntsville, I need somebody to watch my shop for me anyway."

I accepted the offer, and the next thing I knew I was in the gourd shop processing credit card purchases and managing the cash register, running to make some pots, and then running back to receive money for the customers' purchases. And finally one day it dawned on me, "Hey! Wow! My memory is working!"

I was partly functioning from old memories of how to run a business, having owned restaurants and so on. And then I was partly functioning from new, fresh memories that had to do with, for example, the writing out of tickets for purchases. Or there was the having to remember that I was making pottery just prior to rushing to the check-out counter so I would know to return to my pottery-making when I was through receiving payment for purchases. Things were catching on, and the pace was picking up. It had been a couple of years since I took that pottery class, and it had probably been six months since my husband had asked me to start selling my pottery.

People were just coming from everywhere. And I was now making mugs with logos of the bank or business or sports team, and so on, that my customer represented. For a certain bank, for example, the customer would bring me the logo on a business card, and I would freehandedly draw out the logo and craft it onto the mugs.

If I did fifty mugs—and I was doing as much as a hundred a day—I would freehandedly craft the logo onto each mug. There was no pattern, but doing this repetitively made it not as challenging. Nevertheless, I was someone who had commented to my friend just two years earlier, "But I don't have any artistic ability. I can't draw a stick man."

I was getting to be quite the potter. And one day the teacher who had taught me those initial pottery classes walked into the shop. She walked over and picked up one of my mugs, and said, "This is way too heavy."

And she didn't stop with that remark. She hadn't even warmed up. She added, "And just look at the runs on that! Valinda, you don't have any business being in a shop. And you sure don't have any business calling yourself a potter. You're just not good enough. And in ten years you just *might* be able to call yourself a potter."

In response, I simply said, "Well, you know it doesn't really matter what people call me. They can just call me dirt or mud or clay or whatever they want to call me. What matters is that people like my pots, and they just keep buying them as fast as I can make them."

And then I added, "And if you wouldn't mind, would you just leave my shop and not come back again?"

Chapter 20

I HUNG THE SHINGLE!

AFTER I HAD been selling my pottery at my friend's shop for about three years I had to stop because of complications that arose from a surgery I had undergone. Major, major physical complications were to result in my not getting to reopen my shop for another sixteen years. Actually, my husband and my son closed down my pottery business while I was in the hospital. And it remained closed for all those years. And that surgery and the complications that resulted from that surgery are another story, which is found in chapters 23 through 28. But for now, I will skip over that time period and pick up where I resumed making pottery those many years later.

I had started making pottery again but resorted to doing so at my house in a little workshop I had set up. Prior to this I had my wares placed for sale in different shops around town, but the proprietors who were selling my products were asking for forty percent of what I made. I was doing all the work, and they were getting forty percent for carrying my products—and I was having a hard time with that. "There's something about this that's not right," I thought, as I calculated how I couldn't possibly come out ahead because I was already selling my items at such a very reasonable price.

So, I tried to secure a shop of my own in the area where I had a shop before, and there wasn't anything available. And then I began to consider the location where I lived, on the side of the mountain right next to the highway. I wondered, What would happen if I just hung out a shingle here at the house? I wondered if people would come, because I have a long winding driveway. In addition, this involved closing in my front porch to use as the showroom, and the shoppers would have to park behind the house, walk back around front, come up two flights of stairs, and then come into this little front porch area where they would be on top of each other shopping.

But I did it—I hung the shingle! And the people came and kept coming and kept coming and kept coming. The showroom and shopping area were literally so small that the shoppers would have to scoot over and say to the other shoppers, "OK, you can come over here now." They would have to scrunch to make room for each other. I reckoned that they must really want to come if they were willing to go through that kind of trouble to get in there and then the extra trouble required to move around to do their shopping.

To make a long story short, we expanded five times in four years. I turned the shop where I was actually making my pottery into a showroom, and then I later expanded that. I then set up another showroom, and that proved to not be big enough. We were realizing a one-hundred-percent increase every single year for four years, and were just busting at the seams. When the last location was overrun with pottery, we separated the manufacturing area from the same facility housing the showroom, making our four-car garage the showroom area, which made it extra hard on me because I had to run back and forth between those two buildings, which were quite a distance apart. But, as I stated, in four years we expanded five times, and we had a one-hundred-percent increase *every single year*—a hundred percent increase in sales.

And they tell me that our economy is in a recession, so I don't know how we'll be able to make enough pots whenever we get out from under this recession. I have seven employees now, and we still can't keep up with production. We cannot make enough products.

With seven employees and the showroom of our business housed in our four-car garage, we need to expand right now. We've outgrown that facility. And rather than be so far up that hill, my desire is to locate down closer to the road.

We have a sign on the interstate as being a tourist attraction. I am told by Dekalb County's tourist director that we are the number-one tourist attraction there. Whether it is merely to boost my morale or not, he tells me that just the same. We are open seven days a week, and we do have a number of buses carrying church groups and the such coming all the time. The buses have difficulty climbing that hill up our winding driveway and then getting turned around to come back down. But they still come. And we tour the people through the whole facility and show them how the pottery is made from start to finish.

With Miracle Pottery & Art Gallery offering functional, decorative, and affordable pottery, on the functional side there is more than one item that we're kind of famous for. We're making our bacon cookers a hundred at a time and can't keep them in stock. In approximately one minute per slice of bacon, you can enjoy crispy bacon at its best. Our egg scrambler is complete with instructions for adding to one egg all the delectable ingredients you like in your omelet, and breakfast is ready in about thirty to forty-five seconds with no butter or oils needed. We have chicken bakers, custom-made dinnerware sets, and more—all food, microwave, and oven safe.

Our unique, one-of-a-kind decorative selections include vases, angel oil lamps (which can be filled with aromatic scented oils), and stone-faced crowd-pleaser pots—all intricately and beautifully glazed in earthen and nature-inspired hues and tones.

But even our bacon cookers and egg scramblers are beautiful pieces of art, covered in glazes of the richest and most vibrant hues. Ceramic art has this quality of being both functional and beautifully decorative, even when it comes to the simplest objects. So when times are hard and people have to, more than ever, be able to justify their spending, they can have a beautiful piece of art, for example, in a bacon cooker that's eye-catching as it simply sits on the kitchen counter as a gorgeous ceramic pot. Spending money on something that is quite functional while stunning as a piece of art can be justified.

I have a very unique piece of pottery in the shop that is a large, urn-like container with a sizeable jagged-edged hole on one side. And there is a person of clay inside that urn, gazing out through that hole and holding onto its edges with her hands, as if she is the one who has produced that aperture in an attempt to bust out. That person kind of favors me, and intentionally. She depicts this piece of art's descriptive name, "Breaking Free." It is indeed a self-portrait of me, of the artist that was trapped in the body of that woman in the corporate world. The artist was in me all the time, trying to get out. I just didn't know. This is actually the fourth one of these that I've made. The others have sold. I have such a price on this one that I pray nobody is willing to pay it, because I don't want to sell it.

Visitors often ask about a certain painting. In addition to making pottery, I paint. God miraculously gave me the ability to do so, even to paint life-sized murals. And remember, I couldn't draw a stick man. God inspires my paintings, and they are almost always completed in a single sitting. Visitors will ask about a certain painting in our shop or a certain piece of art, especially the urn with the woman's face looking out through the hole. And that opens the door for my employees to tell them the story behind these. A frequently-asked question is, "How did this pottery shop get started, or why did you name it Miracle Pottery?" And there are several reasons why I named it such, with the number one reason, of course, being that it is a miracle that I'm even able to make pottery. But "Miracle" just happens to be my last name.

With every piece of pottery we sell, we include a folded card that has instructions on the inside for the pottery's proper care. And on the backside of the card we have printed, "As long as this pottery is in your possession, you will always have a miracle." On the bottom of each piece of pottery is engraved, "Miracle," along with the emblem of a cross, which is our way of giving God the glory first. We pray over each piece, asking God to bless who receives it, not who buys it but whoever receives it, because much of our pottery is purchased to be given as a gift. People will especially remember us at Christmastime, and with our free gift-boxing and wrapping we ship lots and lots of pottery all over the country.

Chapter 21

FROM NEWSPAPER ARTICLE TO A MAJOR TELEVISION NETWORK STORY

A FELLOW FROM THE local newspaper in our area called me up one day and said, "Mrs. Miracle, we're doing articles on the local businesses here from the perspective of how the devastating economy has had an effect on small businesses."

And I said, "Well, you've called the wrong person."

He asked, "What do you mean?"

I responded, "Well, we've had a one-hundred-percent increase in sales every year."

"*This* year?" he asked.

And I replied, "Yes, sir, we've had a one-hundred-percent increase. Well, actually it was a one-hundred-twelve-percent increase, year to date, this month."

In disbelief, he responded, "You're kidding me."

And I said, "No, sir."

On the other end of the line I heard a quick, "Well, thank you very much." And the phone went *click*.

I turned to my employees and said, "Oh, well, I guess I busted his bubble. He was wanting to write some bad news, and I didn't have any for him."

In a little while the phone rang again, and I recognized the number that came up as the local newspaper calling again. I thought, "Well, they're calling back. Maybe they're not too mad at me."

Telephoning this second time, the fellow asked, "Mrs. Miracle, can we come up there and bring a photographer to take pictures of you making pottery?"

I agreed to do so, and the newspaper personnel came. They photographed me making a couple of pots, and then they just left, not saying a thing. Shortly thereafter I received yet another call saying, "Mrs. Miracle, we'd like to interview you."

Again I agreed, and during the interview one of several questions was in regard to, to what I attributed my success. I explained, "Well, I attribute my success to God. This business belongs to Him, and we give Him all the credit.

All increase that comes is due to Him. He sends the people; He's prospered this business. It's all due to God."

I specifically asked to see the article before it went to press and was told that I would. But that didn't happen, so when the article came out it read, "Mrs. Miracle contributes her great success to her great marketing ability."

I was furious, because I neither stated nor inferred to that reporter that day anything about my having great marketing ability. I had no desire to take credit for what God was doing. I was steaming furious, because I don't steal God's glory. It's His. What Miracle Pottery is today is what *He* made it. Anyone who knows my story from the beginning knows that I absolutely did not have the ability to bring this about. It was God's doing.

But just to show how God can turn the table on a situation, the very next day I got a phone call from a major television network. I later found out that one of my customers had called this TV station and told them, "This girl's got a story. You need to get up there and do a story about her."

The gentleman on the other end of the line exclaimed, "Why, I hear you have quite a story!" And he asked, "Can we come and do a story about you?"

I said, "Why yes, sir, I do have quite a story, but I'm not interested."

Startled, this fellow asked me if I had heard him correctly in that he was from a major television network.

I said, "Yes, sir, I'm not hard of hearing." And I repeated, "But I'm just not interested."

And he, still startled, asked, "Why wouldn't you be?"

"Well, I just had the local newspaper do an article on me. And if I let you do an article on me, I will have to tell you about God, and you'll bleep it all out." I continued, "I'm not interested in doing an article about Valinda Miracle. I'm just not interested at all."

And then I proceeded to tell him how the local newspaper had handled the interview it did of me, how what was printed was untruth, and that I just wasn't interested in that happening again. I told this television network representative, "I give God all the credit for this business, and that's why it is such a success—it's His business, not mine."

And he asked, "Mrs. Miracle, if I promise you that I will not bleep out what you say about God, may I have the privilege of coming and doing your story?"

I sternly said, "If you promise me, if you'll give me your word and you're a man of your word. I don't know you, but if you're a man of your word and you promise me, you can do it. But otherwise you can't."

And he assured me, "I promise you, and I am a man of my word."

So he came with his cameraman, and both were genuinely nice. And when this fellow's interview of me aired, he included everything that I said about God. He had made sure that everything I said about God was in there.

My story on TV wasn't just local news. It was made available to other affiliates of this television network, as well. And it was played over and over, more times than originally intended.

Chapter 22

NOT JUST A BUSINESS BUT A MINISTRY

I DON'T WANT PEOPLE to think that I'm some religious fanatic. I don't get up on a soapbox and try to cram God down anyone's throat. But I do give God the credit where it is due, and Miracle Pottery wouldn't even be in existence if it weren't for Him. I wouldn't even be making pottery if it were not for Him. I'd still be sitting on a couch watching dead fish float in the aquarium; that's where I would be. I wouldn't be in a pottery shop that has a one-hundred-percent increase in sales every year—*during a recession*. I wouldn't be there and have seven super amazing employees.

I have been enabled to take people who've never touched a piece of clay and, in teaching them how to make pottery, give them a purpose. God does that kind of thing! I am only an instrument in it all—and even then only because He touched this piece of clay and gave it purpose.

I have been enabled to take in homeless people and give them jobs. More than one person I have hired knew what it was to go hungry. I feed my employees all the time. I'm always cooking up something and feeding them.

On one occasion—when I actually did not need another potter in the shop, when I had all the employees that I needed—the Lord spoke to my spirit and said that I needed to call such-and-such pottery supply place, that there was someone who needed a job, and that I was to hire him.

And I said, "Lord, I don't really need anybody."

He said, "You call!"

I said, "But, Lord, I'm full up; I don't need anybody."

And He said, "Call!"

And I called. I asked the lady who answered the phone, "Do you know somebody who's needing a job?" I told her that my potter was going to be leaving and going back to Texas, so I was going to be needing someone in the future. That's the only thing I knew to tell her, because I didn't really need anybody right then and my potter did want to return to Texas someday.

And I told that lady, "I'd like to get somebody to train so when my potter goes back to Texas I'll have someone."

And she said, "Well, as a matter of fact, I do." And she told me this person's name.

To make a long story short, Miracle Pottery hired this fellow who had been living in an abandoned bus and put him in an apartment, including getting all the furnishings he needed and filling his pantry with groceries.

Remember the pottery teacher who initially taught me that course on pottery but did not think I could make it as a potter? Well, she came into my shop after I had hired this used-to-be homeless potter whose work had been highly esteemed in days gone by. "Oh, I hear so-and-so is working here!" my former pottery teacher commented.

I responded with a yes, and she said, "Well, you might make it now. You've got yourself a *good* potter."

Now, I had, had my shop for several years by that time, and entire busloads of people were pouring into my place. And still this teacher was walking in and saying, "You *might* make it because you just hired this potter," though this man had been with me only three months of those years, and I, myself, had been making pots for about twenty-three years.

I continue to stand in awe at the number of lives that have been touched through the ministry that goes on at Miracle Pottery. It is not just a pottery shop; it's a mission outreach where people can come to receive ministry and be fed the Word of God. We are open seven days a week because the weekends are the only time that many people from across the country can come here. But I also go into other churches sharing my story. Sometimes my husband goes with me, but often I will go alone to minister at women's conferences and other events. I often take my potter's wheel and demonstrate the art of making pottery as I tell my story, or I will have one of my employees go with me to make pots while I give my story. The Word of God is shared.

On one occasion my husband and I were received with tremendous warmth and graciousness by an Indian church, its congregation made up of those from India or of Indian descent. I had met the pastor and his wife when they came into Miracle Pottery one day. They heard me share my testimony and asked, "Oh, can you please come to our church?"

When I hesitated to respond, the husband said, "You're thinking we're Hindu, aren't you?"

And I confessed, "I'm guilty," because *I did*. And it's not that I wouldn't have gladly shared my testimony to those of Hindu faith; I was merely caught off-guard when someone I thought to be a Hindu asked me to do so.

And he said, "No, we're born-again, Holy Ghost filled!" And they're my dear friends now. And when I had heart surgery (chapters 30 through 32), they came to the hospital and brought me Indian food. The wife worked at the hospital, and she'd come every morning at six o'clock, get my mug that I had brought from my pottery shop, and go fill it with coffee for me.

I've been making pots for about twenty-six years now. Even during those sixteen years when my shop was closed down, I still continued making pottery.

PART VI

THE BIG MIRACLE

Chapter 23

GET YOUR HOUSE IN ORDER!

REMEMBER, I CLOSED my pottery shop for sixteen years because of physical complications. It was during this time that what I call the *big* miracle took place.

I went into the hospital for a scheduled surgery—actually two minor, laparoscopic surgeries, to be performed back to back while I was still under anesthesia. One was for a gallbladder removal and the other for a bladder tack. One doctor was to remove my gallbladder, and then another doctor was to come in behind him and, by way of the same incision, do a bladder tack.

While understandably one might feel at least a little uneasy about something like this, I was feeling a great deal uneasy. I was not unfamiliar with being in a hospital setting and having my body worked on, and I hadn't been told that there was any anticipation of complications with the scheduled procedures. However, this time I sensed the Lord telling me again and again, "Get your house in order. Get your house in order."

I wasn't quite sure what He meant by that, but I thought, "Well, if something were to happen, I'd better get things taken care of."

Wouldn't you think that if you were hearing, "Get your house in order?" an obvious thing to do was make sure you had written your will? So that's what I did. Because of time, this wasn't professionally done—just handwritten. But, I did take this document down to the local bank the day before my surgery and have it notarized.

So, I just wasn't feeling good about things when I left for the hospital bright and early that particular day. It must have been five o'clock in the morning when my husband and I headed out. I so clearly remember looking over at Bill and saying, "Bill, let's take a detour."

And he, looking over at me like I had absolutely lost my mind yet with kindness in his voice, said, "Sweetheart, there is no detour to take between here and there."

My reply was, "Oh, I mean by way of Niagara Falls."

He exclaimed, "Niagara Falls!"

I said, "Yeah, let's just take a big detour by way of Niagara Falls, because I really don't want to do this today."

We had a good laugh, and it seemed to ease my tension a little. After all, I told myself, "Everything is going to be alright. It is only a microscopic gall-bladder removal and bladder tack, two to three hours in surgery, twenty-three hours of observation, and then I'll be going back to my cozy little mountain home. And people are praying for me, and I'm in God's hands."

In looking back, what I was actually getting from the Lord was that every-thing was *not* going to be alright. From what I was hearing Him say—"Get your house in order"—to the uneasiness I was feeling in my spirit, to the sug-gested detour that came out of my mouth from seemingly nowhere, some-thing I had not even been thinking about, it was clear everything was not going to be alright. If I could have heard from the Lord then like I can today, I would have told my husband, "Let's call this thing off."

As it happened, we continued on to the hospital. Twenty-eight days and six surgeries later, as my life was weighing in the balance, I was being prepared for yet another surgery, having many complications, including a puncture in my intestine and also in my bladder that resulted in what is called peritonitis. I had had to have eighteen inches of my intestine removed and two surgeries on my bladder to repair the holes in it.

In addition, I had contracted the most deadly, fastest growing bacterial dis-ease known to man—necrotizing fasciitis, better known as the flesh-eating disease. The tissue becomes extremely hot, swollen, oozing, and then dies. There is no known cause or cure and no treatment except to cut away the dead tissue in an attempt to stop the spread of the disease to the entire body. This can happen within a twelve to twenty-four hour period. I was now in the twentieth hour.

It was supposed to have been two *minor* surgeries. The first one went fine—the gallbladder removal, which also involved a biopsy of my liver. The latter was done because I had suffered terrible headaches as a result of the closed head injury I had received five years ago, and the medication prescribed for that had damaged my liver.

The biopsy turned up gray, which was a matter of concern—so much so that the doctor who performed the first surgery told my gynecologist, the doctor who was to perform the next one, "You might not want to do micro-scopic surgery; it didn't look good in there. She had a lot of adhesions. You might want to open her up."

In response to this, my gynecologist said, "Well, I promised her that I would do the microscopic surgery."

I had undergone surgery years before this—a partial hysterectomy—even before the accident resulting in the closed head injury and had experienced adverse reactions resulting in near death. The attending surgeon told me then that if anybody ever opened me up again he was to be called first, because he had experienced difficulty due to adhesions. My gynecologist, before doing the bladder tack, did call that surgeon, and came back into the room white as a sheet afterward.

I remarked, "You look pretty white, doc. What's wrong?"

He said, "Well, the doctor who performed your hysterectomy told me some things that I'm not real happy about, but I'm going to go ahead and do the surgery."

And so he went ahead, but when he got in there, my bladder had grown to my abdomen wall on one side, and it was grown to my intestine on the other side. So he had to literally peal my bladder off my abdomen wall and peel it off my intestine on the other side, leaving weakened places in my bladder and intestine. The doctor then decided to go back into my abdomen to make sure that there were no leakages anywhere as a result of the weak places, which he knew would eventually heal. He found no leakages; everything was fine. However, rather than the bladder tack concluding my two minor surgeries, several more surgeries were to come.

Chapter 24

A NEGLIGENT DOCTOR AND THE
FLESH-EATING DISEASE

I T HAPPENED TO be the Fourth of July weekend, with the majority of the doctors away from the hospital. On call was this one doctor who was treating my liver. Wanting to run some more tests in this area, he came in immediately after the bladder tack surgery and gave me enemas and laxatives, which resulted in both my intestine and my bladder being punctured where they were weak. From that, I got peritonitis.

Specifically, "peritonitis is an inflammation of the peritoneum, the thin tissue that lines the inner wall of the abdomen and covers most of the abdominal organs." It "may be localized or generalized, and may result from infection (often due to rupture of a hollow organ...)." This "disruption of the peritoneum...may also cause infection simply by letting micro-organisms into the peritoneal cavity."[1] In my case there was a perforation of the intestinal and bladder organs at the location of their weakened walls due to the trauma induced by those carelessly prescribed laxatives and enemas.

The resulting symptoms included abdominal pain and tenderness and fever. The hospital personnel quit telling me what my temperature was after 107 degrees. I was placed on a refrigerated bed, having a refrigerated unit beside it, and packed in ice all over. Oh, I thought I would die! I thought I would die! That's why even to this day I can't stand for anyone around me to be cold.

It was horrible! My teeth chattered, and I so desperately begged the doctor for a blanket that he went and got one, a *warm* blanket, and put it over me. And then he went right down the hall and had the nurse come and take it back. He's the doctor who did the bladder tack, not the one who gave me the enema. He did not find out until later what that other doctor had done. And when he did, he had that doctor, at our instructions, thrown out of my room.

Peritonitis, depending on the severity of it, can be fatal.[2] And if that isn't bad enough, I did not have fluid leaking out of *one* organ but two. I had a hole in my intestine and a hole in my bladder—allowing for micro-organisms in the fluids from each to leak out into my body and to mix. And those fluids were not made to mix. Infection resulted, creating an excruciating burning sensation.

One thing led to the next. I got an abscess on my side. Again, with it being the Fourth of July weekend and very few doctors available, a physician who did not know me and all that was going on was called to help with this new development. He walked in and pinched that abscess, causing its content to flow out onto the floor, and then he left me lying there in that condition for about two hours. I ended up contracting necrotizing fasciitis— better known as the flesh-eating disease. As I stated earlier, it's the fastest growing bacterial disease known to man. It can consume you within twelve to twenty-four hours.

The flesh-eating disease "is a rare condition in which bacteria destroy tissues underlying the skin."[3] This abnormal tissue death, called necrosis, spreads rapidly. "Although the term is technically incorrect, flesh-eating disease is an apt descriptor: the infection *appears* to devour body tissue."[4] Actually, the bacteria do not eat the tissue. They cause the destruction of skin and muscle by releasing toxins.[5]

The infection began locally at the site of the trauma, which in my case was where the walls of my intestine and bladder were perforated. Intense pain and signs of inflammation, including redness and hot, swollen skin came quickly, requiring monitoring in an intensive care unit. Blisters formed, followed by necrosis or death of the tissues beneath the skin. Fever, diarrhea, and vomiting came with the package, as well.[6]

Sometimes necrotizing fasciitis can be contracted through a spider bite.[7] Regardless of how it is acquired, if you get it, for example, on your little finger, the little finger might have to be removed, then the hand, then the arm, and so on, in an attempt to keep the disease from spreading to your entire body. This is the only cure available—surgically cutting away the infected tissue—to keep this monster from spreading. And then this normally leaves a large open wound, which often requires skin grafting.[8]

I was told that I would have to have surgery every day until...

"Till what?" my husband interrupted.

And the doctor answered, "Until *it's* gone or *she* is."

Because of the peritonitis, I had, as I mentioned before, eighteen inches of intestine removed, as well as a hole in my bladder repaired. I was surgically opened in order to have saline solution poured in to wash out all that had leaked into my system, and then I was repacked three times a day. You could hear me scream for three floors, and this went on for three months.

A third hole was found in my bladder, and a catheter was inserted with a diameter larger than that of the hole in order to keep the bladder from leaking any further. You don't even want to try to imagine how uncomfortable that was.

With the necrotizing fasciitis initially attacking in the abdomen, eighteen inches of my intestine along with a large flap of abdominal muscle had to be surgically removed, and by the next day the disease had spread down my left leg and up under my left arm. I had at this point endured several surgeries, and a whole team of doctors were simply waiting for an operating room in which to perform yet another surgery. Ultimately the only course of action would be to remove my left leg and arm and all infected body tissue in between, including any vital organs that had been affected. I remember being so weak that it took every ounce of energy that I had to merely raise my eyelids to see.

Chapter 25

OUT OF THE MOUTH OF BABES

A MOST AMAZING VERSE in the Bible is found in Psalm 8:2, and it is written particularly beautifully in the King James Version: "Out of the mouth of babes and sucklings hast thou ordained strength because of thine enemies, that thou mightiest still the enemy and the avenger." If I didn't understand what that verse meant before I contracted peritonitis and then the flesh-eating disease, I do now. I was to discover its meaning on a day of awaiting yet another surgery.

A family from the church I was attending came to visit. The husband and wife, along with my husband, were standing at the foot of my bed. For some reason, my senses had come to be magnified. I could smell people as they walked down the hospital hall. I could smell their cologne. I could hear the whispering going on at the foot of my bed. I heard every word that was said. Funeral arrangements were being made for me. My husband was telling the visiting couple that I probably wouldn't make it out of this next surgery, that the doctors had already told him that I probably wouldn't survive this one.

But that visiting couple had a little boy, somewhere around two and a half to three years old, and he had a speech problem; he didn't speak well. I had attended church with his dad and mom and sat right behind them. I knew about this baby even before he was out of his mother's womb and even helped pray him into the world.

Well, this child had wandered away from his parents, as children will do, and had come up to my bed. I was turned over on my left side, and he had come up to the right side with his little eyes just barely able to see over the top of the bed because it was elevated so high.

He kept punching my leg. Fortunately it was not the one where the disease had spread. He just kept punching and punching and punching my leg. And I remember taking all the energy that I could muster to simply roll my head over to the right where that little boy was and to weakly ask, "What do you want, darling?"

Now, just in case you don't believe in the prayers of children, let me encourage you to always pay attention to little children when they pray. When I asked this child, "What do you want, darling?" he folded his little hands together, and he answered me only as clearly as he could manage, "I pray for you. I pray for you. OK! I pray for you."

And I said, "OK, darling. OK."

And I didn't understand one word of that baby's mumbled prayer, but I know God did. I know He heard every word because I felt His power come over me. That child could hardly talk. He was enrolled in a speech therapy program. And amidst all of that mumbling, God heard and distinguished every word he prayed. I'll never forget it as long as I live. Daddy and Mom were standing at the foot of my bed, along with my husband, "burying" me, making my funeral arrangements, and that baby was praying for me. It was something to hear and behold!

Chapter 26

THE ANGEL OF THE LORD

THE COUPLE HAD left with their little boy. Everyone had left of the room. With an operating room still not available, I must have drifted off into some unconscious kind of state. Because of what happened next, I'm not convinced that I hadn't died lying right there in my bed.

I heard the words, "Breathe, Valinda. Breathe!"

I managed to barely open my eyes to see and then my mouth to breathe, and when I did there was a loud noise. If you've ever had your lungs collapse, you are familiar with the sound of the air as it comes rushing back in because your lungs had completely emptied.

I remember thinking, "Wow! I wonder how long it's been since I breathed last. Obviously my lungs collapsed, because they're filling back up."

And then I contemplated, "That wasn't one of the doctors I heard, and that wasn't one of the nurses. That wasn't even the family, but somebody's there."

I had heard, "Breathe, Valinda. Breathe," coming from a particular direction, and when I opened my eyes even farther to look that way, there before me was the most divine, illustrious sight I had ever seen—the Angel of the Lord in all of His glorious splendor, wondrously arrayed in a robe of dazzling, brilliant white! As if the very sun itself was being eclipsed by His presence—such was the golden, streaming, luminous glow radiating from behind where Jesus stood. I could not actually see His face, just the outline, and could only discern the shape of His head. Only His silhouette was distinguishable. I could see His hair, like baby's ringlets, hanging down, draping His shoulders and onto His chest, and because of that exuding, powerfully luminous glow framing His being those ringlets had the appearance of spun gold.

To look in Jesus's direction was to attempt to gaze upon the blazing sun—it was blinding. Had the light not have come from behind, I wouldn't have been able to look upon Him at all. And even then I had to tilt my head in order to make out as much of His physique as I did. Focusing with as much intensity as I could muster, I could not see His hands; I could see no further down than mid-chest.

And we—Jesus and I—conversed, but not in the normal human way. I wasn't hearing Him with my natural ears; I was hearing Him with my heart—just like I do now when He speaks to me. And when I talked to Him, I didn't have to say a word. I made no utterances with my mouth or vocal cords. All I had to do was think. And just as soon as my question became a thought, just as soon as it entered my mind, He answered me. And then I would have another thought, and He would answer me. And I'd have another thought, and He would answer me. He answered *every* question I had. I believe this is what David was describing when he said, "You perceive my thoughts from afar" (Ps. 139:2).

And when it was over, I was at peace. My Lord stayed there as long as I needed Him—until I was at *total* peace, convinced that whatever happened, I would be OK. And while still facing me, He simply began to ascend until He exited up and out of the corner of the room, right through the ceiling. And then the hospital personnel came rushing in to get me for surgery.

Chapter 27

A TRIP TO HEAVEN

SOMETIME IN BETWEEN being wheeled into surgery and waking up in my room afterward, I had two large angels escort me into an inner chamber of heaven. When we arrived my attention was drawn to an even larger chamber to my left, where glorious, golden light was emanating and bursting in every direction from the doorway, lighting up everything around. Somehow I knew that was where the source of life was, and that's where I wanted to go, because I knew that the source of life was my heavenly Father.

But the angels held me back and said, "No, you can't go just yet."

I exclaimed, "Oh, but that's where my Lord is! My Lord is there, and that's where I want to go!"

I was told, "No, you can't go just yet. We've got to show you some things."

I then looked over to my right in this chamber that we were in, and there was a huge vessel. It wasn't like anything I'd ever seen, so the best way I can describe it is to call it a vessel. It was a voluminous, submarine-shaped object, shiny, like stainless steel, but I'm sure I was looking at an encasement of the purest white gold. As people—just ordinary people—stood all around, an iridescent, predominately blue, and sizeable light instantaneously appeared in this thing, this vessel. And when it did, those people jubilantly danced and clapped and shouted, "There's another one coming in! There's another one coming in! Just look! There's another one coming in!" They were *so* excited!

"I don't understand," I told the angels.

And one of them responded, "Well, come, and we'll show you what Jesus *sees* and *feels*."

"Oh, that would be wonderful!" I exclaimed.

And suddenly we were back on Earth in a large city like Chicago or New York or someplace where there was just a sea of people walking on the sidewalks. And the angels showed me this one lady moving along. For the purpose of sharing my story, I will call her Miss Full-of-Pain. I not only somehow perceived that she was sad and heartbroken, absolutely crying out with suffering and pain, but I could literally *feel* her torment, to the extent that I myself doubled over with pain because hers was so great.

The angels informed me that this is what Jesus sees and feels. And I said,

"Surely He doesn't feel this kind of pain. Surely He's suffered enough that He doesn't have to suffer this kind of pain—and from the *entire* human race!"

"There's not a tear shed or a pain felt that He doesn't see or feel," the angel explained.

And then I was shown another lady who was coming in the opposite direction toward the first lady. And for the sake of description, I will call her Miss Sunshine, because she was absolutely radiant, stepping lively steps, and oozing with the love of Jesus. You could *see* the love of Jesus pouring out of her, and I *felt* that as well. It just went all through me and warmed my soul.

And I was told, "Jesus feels this, too."

"Well, maybe it's not so bad if He gets to trade off some of the bad for the good," I concluded.

And then it was obvious that Miss Full-of-Pain and Miss Sunshine were going to cross paths. And when they did, Miss Sunshine looked over at Miss Full-of-Pain and gave her the simplest smile, not even showing her teeth as she did. And I *felt* that smile go all through the lady who was in pain. Its warmth and love radiated all through her, all the way to her toes—because she needed that smile so badly. She just needed to know that someone somewhere cared about her.

And suddenly the two angels and I were back in that chamber, an inner chamber of heaven, just in time to see another one of those lights show up in that vessel. And again those people joyously and exuberantly danced and clapped and reverently shouted, "There's another one coming in!"

And puzzled once more, I stated, "I still don't understand."

The angel responded, "That's that kind deed being stored up."

"What kind deed?" I asked.

"The kind deed she did," the angel said, referring to Miss Sunshine's smile.

"But that wasn't a kind *deed*," I determined. "She didn't do anything but smile."

And then I heard a great voice coming from the source of the light, from the source of that great golden glow I had seen emanating from the doorway of that even larger inner chamber, which I had perceived to have been the throne room of God. It was my Lord, and He was speaking my name and in an utterance that saturated the very air and everybody around with life, vitality—*pure* energy. How can I describe it? It was like the sound and feel of splashing, invigorating rushing water—but way more. I can think of nothing that comes even close to describing the experience of hearing His words. It was living. It was living word that came from Him. That must have been what He was trying to tell us in John 6:63, "The words I have spoken to you are spirit and they are life," or in Hebrews 4:12, "For the word of God is living and active."

And at the sound of my name, I fell to my knees. "Valinda," my Lord said, "this is what you must go back and tell My people. You're all waiting around on Me to give you a great commission to do, and all I've ever wanted was for you to love Me and love each other and show acts of kindness one to another. That's *all* I've ever wanted."

And then He showed me—like a brief video clip—my youngest son, and He said, "He still needs you, Valinda."

And when the Lord planted that thought about my son, causing my heart to sadden as I was made aware that my son still needed me, I was out of there, because there is no sorrow in heaven. The instant my heart saddened for my son, I was on my way back to Earth.

I saw my body lying on the hospital bed, and I slipped right back into it through the top of my head, just like slipping a hand into a glove. Two male nurses were in the room—one named Phillip and the other named Michael. And whenever I opened my eyes, they, with mouths agape, slammed back against the bathroom door, making a terrible noise.

I asked, "Why are you looking so frightened? What's wrong?"

One of them answered, "Well, uh, well, you, you've been mighty sick."

I said, "Yes, I know, but I'm better now. And let me tell you the good news: we've been so disillusioned focusing on this sin and that sin and this church and that church and all this other stuff when it comes to God. And none of it means a thing when it comes right down to it, and especially not in comparison to God's only real desire for us—which is for us to love Him and love one another and show acts of kindness one to another. Nothing else really matters."

Religion is not going to reach the world. This message will.

Chapter 28

THE BANDAGES ARE REMOVED

PRIOR TO THIS surgery, the doctors had made it known that there was a great chance I would not survive. My family members had been called in. I had been asked for my living will.

I was told later that when the bandages and packing from the wounds of the necrotizing fasciitis were to be removed, the attending physician said to the other doctors who were present, "Boys, I hate to take these bandages off because it's not a pretty sight. But we'll see what we can do." This surgery had actually involved the removal of a large flap of abdominal muscle. There was concern as to what course of action would have to be taken next since the flesh-eating disease had already attacked the tissue of my left leg and arm.

Removing the bandages, however, the doctor exclaimed, "Oh, look, it's bleeding! Dead skin doesn't bleed! Dead skin doesn't bleed!"

Where the incision on my abdomen had been made during the previous day's surgery, the flesh was bleeding. I was washed out yet another time with saline and repacked. But even more, the skin on my leg and arm had returned to normal and no evidence of the hideous flesh-eating disease could be found. *The bacteria was gone!*

I had to have a total of six surgeries and remained overall in the hospital for twenty-eight days, but to God be the glory. He had been doing a work in my family and me during my illness. That their faith might be increased, many patients were brought to my room for us to tell them what a miracle God had done. One doctor almost left his practice to stay in the room with me. As my husband and sister read from the Book of Psalms, we all prayed and wept. The Ninety-First Psalm was my favorite, and verse 10, especially—"Then no harm will befall you, no disaster will come near your tent."

Following my surgery, I was reassured by my doctor that I had been correctly diagnosed with the flesh-eating disease, that there indeed was no cure for that disease, and that I no longer had that disease. I needed to hear him confirm what I already knew to be true. That doctor came to be a believer through all of this.

He now plays my husband's album in the operating room. One song in particular on that album is called "Fear Not," and was inspired by Isaiah 41:10, which says, "Fear thou not; for I am with thee: be not dismayed; for I am thy God: I will strengthen thee; yea, I will help thee; yea, I will uphold thee with the right hand of my righteousness" (KJV).

PART VII

TO THE MISSION FIELD

Chapter 29

ONLY A SEASON

I LIVED! I SURVIVED a doctor's negligence and the flesh-eating disease. And since then I've made three trips to Honduras in Central America—medical mission trips as a dental assistant.

Next to no one wants to go on a mission trip as a dental assistant (or a dentist, for that matter) because of the danger involved. Countries that are drawing cards for missionaries are often absolutely infested with the AIDS virus, and the dental assistant's job involves, of course, working in the mouths of these victims and being exposed to their body fluids, including their blood.

In these remote, third-world country areas, you have to resort to extracting the teeth because it is rare to have equipment such as drills for filling them. And besides, there is no electricity for operating certain dentistry instruments in many of the locations to which missionaries go. Our particular team had no choice but to extract the teeth, and we did that all day long.

Very often the teeth were broken off at the gum, which is common among AIDS victims, so we had to resort to prying these teeth out, exposing ourselves to teeth bites or the splattering of blood. We wore masks, but we did not wear goggles over our eyes, therefore, exposing our own body fluids to those of the AIDS patients. This was all extremely hazardous health-wise, to say the least.

And while we did wear gloves, we had to give injections, and there was the danger of a needle puncturing the glove and, consequently, the hand. Or we could tear our gloves and nick or slice our hands when we washed instruments that were sharp, and, therefore, be exposed to our patient's body fluids on those instruments.

Nobody under these circumstances really wants to go to the mission field as a dentist or dental assistant, yet there are many who do, and I personally felt led by the Lord to be one of them. I felt like that's what God wanted me to do.

And, oh, how it just broke my heart to have to extract the teeth of the little children. Like I have explained, we were left with no choice. To make it easier on the children, I took a bare minimum of clothing for myself on these trips, and I crammed my suitcase full of stuffed animals. And as these little ones came running up to me and hugged my neck, I gave them a stuffed animal as I set them in the chair to have their teeth worked on. They would put both of their hands around that little animal, and I would then take my hand and place it right over their little hands, because I knew they were about to get an injection in their gums so we could extract their teeth. I needed to hold tight to their little hands to keep them out of their mouths while they were receiving that injection. How the tears would stream down their little faces! Again, my heart was broken.

They were the most beautiful little boys and girls with skin like satin and blue-black hair. I wanted to bring every one of them home with me. But young and old—from children to eighty year olds—they all came. And some of them walked all night to get to where we were—some all day and all night. Often the only available form of transportation was to walk.

Not only were there multiple cases of half of the teeth being broken off at the gum, but there were abscesses as well. And especially among the children this was painful to see. Some teeth only needed to be filled, but we had no way of filling them, so in order to get our patients out of their pain and misery we, of course, had to extract their teeth.

The children would absolutely hug all over me, happy to receive their stuffed animals and happy to be relieved of their pain. Some of the other missionaries half-cautioned and half-ridiculed me, saying, "You ought not let those little kids hug all over you like that. You're going to get lice."

And I replied, "Do you think I'm worried about getting lice? If you're worried about getting lice, you don't need to be here. I'm standing here with my hands in their mouths, and I'm not worried about getting AIDS. Do you think I'm worried about getting lice?" And I added, "God sent me here. I don't know what your purpose is here, but I'm here because God sent me here."

And while all the other dental assistants worked with the American doctors who had come on the trip, I was drawn to a Honduran doctor who was present to take part in this outreach on behalf of his people. He hadn't been given an assistant.

I was told, "He doesn't need anybody. He works by himself."

"How do you know?" I questioned.

"He doesn't need anybody. We don't ever give him anybody. He works by himself," was the reply.

I continued, "Well, what makes you think he doesn't need anybody? He's doing the same work you guys are doing. What makes you think he doesn't need an assistant?"

"Well, he just works by himself!"

"Apparently, he doesn't have a choice," I concluded, and then emphasized, "I will work with him. Ask him if he needs me to work with him."

And the Honduran doctor's response was, "Oh, yes, yes, yes, please work with me!"

And come to find out, he spoke very good English—kind of broken, but very good. And I would get him to interpret for me as I witnessed to every person who sat in that dentist's chair while we were there. I told them about Jesus and won many, many of them to Him.

I would pray for that Honduran doctor. He was just a little bitty guy. He and I would do eight hundred extractions in three days, and this dentist's tiny wrists, I know, felt like they were falling off as he struggled to pry loose and pull teeth that were wrapped around the patient's bone. He cared about his people deeply; that's why he was there. Alongside the missionary team, he struggled so hard to help the natives of his country.

And as he labored so intently, I would pray for those teeth to pop out— "Lord, just let this tooth pop out. Let it be easy for him to get it out. And let the patient be calm. Give him (or her) sweet peace, Lord. And give Dr. George supernatural strength to get this tooth out."

This doctor had a long name that I could not pronounce so I asked him if I could simply call him Dr. George. And I'd say, "Lord, just help that tooth to *pop* out of there. Let it come out with ease." And time and time again that tooth would do just that—pop out and go flying across the room. And Dr. George would get so excited when it did.

When our team would return to their rooms at night, some of those who understood the language would tell me, "Valinda, Dr. George gets so excited, and he goes back to his room and says, 'That lady, that Mrs. Miracle, would pray; and she would say, "Just let it pop out," and it would go *zing* across the room. I want to know her Jesus. I want to know her God.'"

And so every day he would help me interpret. And finally one of our interpreters helped me give my testimony about the flesh-eating disease to Dr. George and to some others there. We gathered all the people together, and we had a testimony service.

And Dr. George said, "Oh, I want to know her Jesus! I want to know her Jesus!"

And that's what happened—he came to know Jesus. I gave the plan of salvation to him, and he said, "Oh, yes, yes, I accept your Jesus. But one problem, one problem—my family is Catholic." And he continued, "I live with my mother and daddy because I don't have money to move out on my own."

I said, somewhat surprised, "But, Dr. George, you're a dentist!"

He explained, "I work in a clinic. I make twenty-five cents an hour. I don't have money to feed my family. My little boy I have to send to school. I don't have money to feed my family."

I repeated, "But you're a dentist!"

"I don't make money," he said.

I discovered that he was getting children's shoes that I had brought from the States to take home to his own child. And he asked me for toys, as well, for his son. He told me, "My little boy doesn't have Christmas. Can I take this to him?"

And I just cried. Here was a dentist, and he couldn't feed his family. And he explained, "When my family finds out that I've accepted your Jesus, they'll put me out of the house. They'll no longer have anything to do with me."

His parents were Catholics who didn't believe in the born-again experience. So he explained, "When they find out I believe in your Jesus, they'll put me out of the house. I'll have no place to live."

And I asked, "Dr. George, you're telling me that you're a dentist, and you don't have enough money to feed your family?"

"Yes," he said.

"We're going to do something about that." I informed him. "I'm going to go back to the States, and we're going to do something about that."

And God prompted me right then and there to help this man. And when I returned to the States, I bought him a Bible first of all—a Spanish NIV Bible that he could understand. And I took it to him on my next mission trip. I also went around and collected dentistry equipment, furniture, and supplies. I was able to acquire an X-ray machine and a dental chair.

Money was supplied to purchase dental instruments in Honduras cheaper than what it would cost to ship them from the States to Dr. George. People gave and gave and gave—from every direction—and they were glad to give. They set that young Honduran man up in a dental practice of his own. He was able to move out of the clinic. He now has a little girl, and his family has been able to move out of his parents' home and have a place of their own. Dr. George is still joining and assisting the Americans when they go to Honduras on these medical missionary trips, and he's winning his people to the Lord at the same time.

I personally have been blessed to work with this impressive man on all three trips that I have taken to his country. I believe that a main purpose for my going to Honduras was to connect with this doctor whom God was going to move for in such a mighty way.

It was on my second trip to Honduras that I almost died. I suffered a heat stroke, which could have been prompted by an already malfunctioning heart. This was before I had the heart surgery I will share about in the chapter to come.

I was asked following the heat stroke, "Valinda, do you know how badly sick you were?"

And I said, "Well, I know it was pretty bad."

And the person telling me this said, "You were so bad that we needed to MedEvac [medical evacuate] you out of here, but we couldn't get you stabilized enough to do it."

All through the night following the stroke, a nurse monitored the IV drips as an attempt was made to get me stabilized so I could be medically evacuated the next day, but when the morning came I was miraculously able to go back to work on the mission field. I have to say, "If God does not call you to a foreign country, you'd better not go—unless your heart's beating out of your chest to do so."

I vividly remember to this day a young Honduran preacher to whom I sent money to help support him and his family. I did so for quite some time. In fact, some other missionaries and I lived with his family on one of our trips. He took us around the area where he lived and into one village in particular that you could only reach by *burro* or walking. And we didn't have a *burro*, so we had to walk. And it was just as well, because getting to that village meant descending a rocky, gravelly, near-vertical mountainside that I would shudder to think of descending astride a *burro*. That mountainside was the only way in and the only way out. There was no so-called path, and we went slipping and sliding all the way down as those gravels rolled out from under our feet.

There was a school in the valley, and that was our headquarters for distributing the medicine that we brought with us. These medicines were chosen for a population for which intestinal worms was a killer problem. And then because the water—found in dirty ditches—was so impure, diarrhea was rampant. These people were dying at a very young age, and they were dying for the lack of simple medications that they couldn't obtain because of lack of transportation or money or simple availability. They didn't even have aspirins. Not only did we distribute medicines but we went door-to-door to deliver the Word of God.

We visited orphanages, and how very much I was moved by the happiness I saw among a people who suffered such adversity. They had smiles on their faces; and they would hug you aggressively, almost wrestling you to the ground. And they were sweet—the sweetest little kids you've ever seen. And, oh, they would beg us to take them home with us.

When possible, we took an old school bus from village to village, and there was great concern about *banditos*, or bandits. We could not wear any jewelry, none at all, and we couldn't carry any money with us anywhere because the *banditos* would stop the bus. And they did stop our bus one time, boarded it with their machine guns, searched all through it, and then let us go. I'm not sure what happened there, but I will admit that we were afraid for our lives. It was a frightening experience.

These *banditos* had a reputation for harassing, hurting, even killing people. They would kill in a heartbeat for a ring on someone's finger. And they thought all Americans were rich, and for the most part we were—when we compared our standard of living to theirs. If they had only known that some of the others and I who were on this trip had to work and have bake sales to raise the money to go, they probably wouldn't have bothered to stop our bus. But the point remains: a person is taking his life into his own hands when he goes somewhere like this.

I knew I was where I was supposed to be. I actually went to Honduras with one church group on one trip and stayed over three weeks longer, along with two other ladies, to return back to the States when another church group's trip concluded. I wanted to stay because I wanted to know more about these people and where and how I could help them.

At that time one of my friends, who was a nurse, and I worked further with this young preacher I previously mentioned, traveling from village to village with him because we wouldn't have been safe on our own. Needless to say, there were no McDonald's or Burger King restaurants. We weren't staying in hotels. We were in villages with no electricity and no running water. We became quite appreciative of baby wipes and hand sanitizer. And real bathrooms and toilet paper would never be taken for granted by us again. We had no toilet paper in Honduras unless we carried it with us. And even if we had it, we couldn't put it in the plumbing if we found a bathroom. There were no toilets with plumbing where we went. There was this little pipe, and it was situated very close to the ground—to a hole in the ground. And that was the toilet.

The idea that many have of going to the mission field is staying in a hotel and doing a little bit of teaching in the villages. They never really stay in the homes and actually live among the people. The homes there were grass huts with maybe a little mud on the sides.

And the schools where we sometimes lodged had tarantulas crawling through them—scorpions and tarantulas. And we'd hear them running around, even on our luggage, at night. We had to be sure and zip our luggage and keep what clothes we were going to put on the next day in a Ziploc bag.

We slept on cots, and we slept under covers at night because after a day of 116 degrees the temperature could drop to 40 degrees after the sun went down. And you couldn't be sure there wasn't something crawling under your covers— like a scorpion or tarantula. If you had to get up in the night, you didn't know what you might step on because it was pitch-black dark.

I wasn't a teenager when I went to Honduras on the first trip. I already had two sons, and they were far from being babies. I was married again, and I was a businesswoman. And it hadn't been long after I had dealt with the flesh-eating disease—maybe a year or two later. Here I was sleeping on a cot in a schoolhouse in the pitch-black night with scorpions and tarantulas around, after I had battled the flesh-eating disease. And, remember, one of the ways to contract the flesh-eating disease is by being bit by a spider—not a scorpion or tarantula, mind you, but it's enough to make one quite apprehensive after having gone through the ordeal I went through fighting this disease.

But instead of the flesh-eating disease causing me to fearfully withdraw in a shell and not ever take chances again, it made me want to make every day count. I had gone through so much in life that I wanted to make *every* day count. I didn't want to miss a thing, and most assuredly I didn't want to miss God. And whatever He said to do, I did it. And I still do.

As far as what my two sons and my husband had to say about me making a trip or trips like this, they just knew that if God called me to do something, I was going to do it. My sons, especially, had grown to accept that.

I returned to Honduras yet a third time—a three-week stay to work with Dr. George once more. Also there was another doctor who needed help, a medical doctor who was living in abject poverty and, like Dr. George, eager to help his people. You see, in Honduras you're either very wealthy or very poor. There is no in-between. Just as I was allowed with Dr. George, I was allowed to be instrumental in furnishing the supplies this doctor needed to do what was in his heart to do, and he, too, hungering for the reality of God, readily accepted His miracles. Helping both these doctors was essentially why God sent me to Honduras. And both are spreading the gospel much more than I could have ever thought of doing, as both speak the language of their people and know their people's heart and needs in a way I didn't and couldn't.

This is why I went to Honduras those three times—to essentially help these two doctors get established in their medical practice and in their ministry—and I haven't had that beating in my heart to ever go back again. I believe there is an important message here about God making you passionate about something and drawing you to do something for only a season, and then you've got to know when that season is up. Just because He calls you to a mission field doesn't mean that it will be a life-long pursuit. It may only be for a certain time, a certain season of your life. And we must be discerning in this respect. I believe that this is sometimes why we have people who are burned out—they are overstaying a particular season as far as their destiny is concerned.

And, along the same line, we've got to be careful to not go and burn all our bridges as we transition from one season of our life to the next, as in thinking, "Well, because I've got to go to the mission field, I must sell everything." Perhaps it will be necessary to do that, as in "sell everything," but perhaps that is not what God is asking you to do. Your time on the mission field may be a temporary thing only.

AIDS, lice, tarantulas, scorpions, *banditos*, a beautiful people who changed my life, two doctors that God wanted to bless, only a season: "There is a time for everything, and a season for every activity under heaven....a time to embrace and a time to refrain" (Eccles. 3:1, 5).

PART VIII

FOR THE SAKE OF OTHERS

Chapter 30

SWIMMING WITH THE DOLPHINS

Ⅰᴛ ᴡᴀs Dᴇᴄᴇᴍʙᴇʀ of 2009. My health kept spiraling down, down, down; and I had been to doctor after doctor after doctor. I could no longer even walk across the floor. This had begun years ago, over twenty years ago, when ascending two flights of stairs had become overly exhausting, then impossible. And then, transpiring gradually over another period of time, having to ascend not only one flight of stairs but even the smallest incline was out of the question. Next, I could hardly walk at all.

Today I so appreciate and enjoy being able to walk like anyone else. But back then, even before my walking had reached its worst, I would struggle along to try to walk like everyone else when we'd go hiking, because I knew I wasn't that old and should be able to do it. But regardless of my positive thinking and positive attitude it was all I could do to try to keep up. I would be so out of breath when I got back to the car that I thought I was going to die. I thought my heart was going to beat right out of my chest, but I wouldn't ever say anything because I hated to complain. However, when I finally found out what the problem was, no one would have faulted me for complaining. I certainly had reason to do so.

I had kept going to doctors, and they had repeatedly checked me and said, "Well, Valinda, your arteries are wide open. You don't have high blood pressure. You know, everything's fine."

Ultimately, it was discovered that I had a mass in my heart the size of which was not clear, but major open-heart surgery was deemed necessary and scheduled for after the holidays. My chest was to be cut open, my lungs and heart taken out, and then a large mass removed from the middle of my heart. Keeping in mind that the aorta conveys the blood from the left ventricle of the heart to all of the body except the lungs, this mass in my heart was blocking my aortic valve. This blockage was obstructing the blood flow to the rest of my body and causing back-flushing. Being left open all the time was my mitral valve—a dual-flap valve in the heart that lies between the left atrium and the left ventricle. To make this simple, the end result was that the blood was just accumulating in my lungs and wouldn't go into any other part of my body. I was literally drowning in my own blood.

With the holidays upon us, my heart surgery was scheduled for afterward to ensure the availability of all the hospital staff necessary to get the job done. My family always gathered home for Christmastime, and I always cooked a big meal. This year was no different, with the exception that I had food catered in for the occasion. I could barely get out of my chair. I could barely get to the bathroom. I could no longer even make it out to my pottery shop. Hardly able to breathe, it was all I could do to get up and fill my own plate at our Christmas dinner. But I made a good appearance, concealing as much as possible of the physical state I was in. We opened all the presents, everyone was having a good time, and everything was going rather smoothly.

Though they had no idea just how badly and how rapidly my health had declined, my children knew I was ill and was scheduled for surgery following the holidays, so much so that they were protective of me when my granddaughter wanted to climb into my lap. She was told, "No, No, Mem Mem's not feeling well. You need to not get up there."

And I said, "Oh, yes, you can get up here, but Mem Mem just can't lift you," because she was six and a little heavy for me to lift at that time.

All the talk about me going into the hospital had concerned Lana. So she crawled up into my lap and, looking right into my eyes, asked, "Mem Mem, are you going to die?"

And I kind of had to check with my Father first before I answered her, because I wanted to be truthful with my granddaughter. Sensing His "OK," I said to Lana, "No, Mem Mem's not going to die." And, as I was further prompted, I stated, "As a matter of fact, Mem Mem's going to have to heal for a while. She's going to have a great big boo boo."

I then showed Lana how far down on my chest the surgical incision would be made. And I asked her, "You know how you get a boo boo on your leg?"

She replied, "Yes."

"Well, Mem Mem's going to have a big boo boo. It's going to come from here to here. But when it gets well—it's going to take a little while for it to get well—but when it gets well, you and I are going to go to Disney World."

And even when I told Lana that she and I were going to Disney World, feeling in my own heart that I would be here to do something like going to Disney with her, I was rolling my eyes, thinking, "We're going to Disney World, Lord? That's a tall order!"

And He whispered in my ear, in that small, gentle voice that is peculiar to Him, "You're going to come through this victorious."

That's all I needed to hear! I then said to Lana, "Yes, we're going to Disney World. Does that sound fine to you?"

And she responded, "Yes, but I don't really like Disney World too much. Can we go see Shamu and swim with the dolphins?"

And I answered, "Yes, we can! Wouldn't we have lots of fun?"

And she exclaimed, "Oh, Mem Mem!" as she hugged me up so sweet. And she added, "I just love the dolphins! I want to be a dolphin trainer when I grow up."

I said, "Well, we'll just go see about learning how to do that!"

Lana was OK after hearing that Mem Mem was going to be alright. And six months later, almost to the day, Lana and I were at Discovery Cove swimming with the dolphins.

I consider myself to have come through the surgery wonderfully, in spite of flatlining four times in the surgery's aftermath—that is to say that four different times on the heart monitor a flat line showed up rather than a moving one, indicating no electrical activity coming from my heart. "Some consider one who has flatlined to be clinically dead, regardless of eventual resuscitation or lack thereof."[1] So, I repeat: I consider myself to have come through remarkably well, especially in light of the fact that some would say I came back from the dead four different times in the course of things. Yes, I came through victorious—just like my Father said I would.

And in the vicinity of six months later, Lana, a teenage friend, and I were on our trip. Here I was—a sixty year old—with a six year old and a nineteen year old and heading off to Sea World. And we went swimming with the dolphins, and we wanted to do everything else that had to do with the water parks.

For close to twenty years I hadn't been able to climb even one flight of stairs, much less two flights of stairs, and eventually the slightest incline was a tremendous challenge. But all of a sudden I found myself up in the tallest tower of those water slides, way up in the air. I imagine it was at least eight stories high. And I had walked all the way up there—many, many, many, many steps. When I looked down and realized what had just been accomplished, I shouted, "Praise You, Lord!" just as loud as I could, because I knew that before the surgery I couldn't have done that. Yes, I say again: I had come through victorious—just like my Father said I would.

And I came down that slide and, along with my granddaughter, swam with the dolphins. I mean, we held on to the dolphins and swam with them. And one dolphin, in particular, just kept coming back to me and nudging me. I don't know if it picked up on anything in regard to what I had gone through. Dolphins are very sensitive, you know.

And I have discovered that dolphins aren't the only animals that are sensitive. My husband had always forbidden me to have animals in the house, but a friend of mine gave me two kittens for Christmas this year. And before she did, I asked her if she was going to do that, because I had already sensed that she was. And she answered my question with a question of her own, "How did you know the Lord spoke to me and told me I was supposed to give you kittens for Christmas?"

The kittens were mine; I got to keep them. And I let them sleep with me that first week because I didn't know how they would fare in their new home. Then something happened that was most meaningful to me. The kittens would wake me up. They would pat my cheek, and placing their noses right by my mouth, they would wake me up. And I truly believe they did this for the purpose of getting me to breathe again. I really think I had stopped breathing, that I was suffering from sleep apnea—"a sleep disorder characterized by abnormal pauses in breathing or instances of abnormally low breathing during sleep."[2] I seriously believe I had stopped breathing and that those kittens were trying to wake me up. They are mine, and they are fabulous—one named Clay and the other named Glaze.

Chapter 31

SHOCKED TO DEATH

WHILE HOLDING LANA on my lap at Christmastime in 2009 the Lord had told me in regard to the upcoming surgery, "You're going to come through this victorious." But when He and I were talking about this later He said, "You're going to come through this victorious, but there are two people who need to see you come through this." As it turned out, these two people were doctors.

The surgery itself went well. Because the sizeable mass that had to be removed was located right in the middle of my heart, where the heart's electrical system was located, scooping out that mass required scooping out much of this electrical system. Therefore, a pacemaker had to be placed on the outside of my body for the surgery and be permanently implanted near the heart afterward. As it turned out the pacemaker that was placed on the outside of my body to keep my heart beating during surgery shorted out while I was in intensive care. It burned me and literally shocked me to death; I flatlined. Once I was resuscitated, I knew that someone simply touching me could cause this to happen again.

So I would forewarn, "Listen, if you touch me, you'll cause me to flatline."

"Well, I've got to do such-and-such," the attending doctor or nurse would say.

I said again, "I'm telling you, if you touch me, you'll cause me to flatline."

"Well, I've got to do such-and-such," he or she would insist again.

"I'm telling you, you can't touch me! You'll cause me to flatline!"

"Well, I've got to do such—"

And, "Congratulations!" I thought afterward. "They did it again!" By then I had flatlined three times.

That pacemaker was lying there right on top of my abdomen, and every time they were touching me it was causing this to happen. Somehow in touching me and the metal bed, for instance, at the same time, it caused me to flatline. Exactly how and why this was taking place I didn't know. It just happened one time too many as far as I was concerned.

Once the permanent pacemaker was in place, the doctor said, "OK, Mrs. Miracle, we've got your permanent pacemaker in; now you're fine."

I said, "No, I'm not! You'd better get the crash cart in here."

"Mrs. Miracle, we have you fixed."

I said, "No, you don't! Get the crash cart in here. We're going again!"

"Mrs. Miracle, you're—"

And about that time, I flatlined *yet again*.

This time I simply felt myself going. I was leaving. I knew that I was leaving. I had been through this enough to know. Four times I had flatlined.

Chapter 32

FORGING A WAY

B UT GOD, WHILE assuring me that I would come through this surgery victorious, had told me that I had to go through it for the sake of two people. "There are two people who need to see you go through this," He had said.

As it turned out, one was the surgeon and one was my cardiologist. Neither had performed this kind of surgery before, and immediately after my surgery they scheduled three other individuals for the same procedure because they now knew that this procedure was what these three individuals needed. I had been the guinea pig (I prefer "the instigator") for a pioneer endeavor that forged the way and cleared a path for others to follow.

When I was told that three others were being scheduled for the same surgery, I laughed as I told my physicians, "Oh, you're going to fix them now! You're not going to let them die slow deaths like you were me!"

Again, these doctors had never performed an operation like this. They hadn't been able to diagnose what was going on with me. They didn't know what was wrong. I explained to them that I couldn't breathe, that I couldn't get across the room without thinking I was smothering to death. So they ran all kinds of breathing tests on me, only to find that this had nothing to do with my lungs.

They performed an arteriogram—an imaging test that uses X-rays and a special dye to see inside the arteries[1]—and my arteries were perfectly clear. No clogged arteries for me. No high blood pressure. I had *no* symptoms of heart disease.

But my husband and I kept insisting that something was wrong, that I had gone from a healthy person to this person who couldn't walk across the room without nearly suffocating, who couldn't get to the bathroom and back without thinking she was dying. My husband had been going to this same cardiologist because he had had a heart attack, and he, the doctor, just wasn't hearing us. Finally my husband grabbed him by his shirt and said, "Listen to me! She's dying, and unless you do something, she's going to die!"

"We can try one more thing," the doctor said. He ordered an echocardiogram, sometimes called a cardiac ECHO, which is a sonogram of the heart. "It uses standard ultrasound techniques to image two-dimensional slices of the heart."[2] I was put to sleep and a probe was run down into my lung to get as close as possible to the heart to see what was going on. A small mass—or what was thought to be a *small* mass—was detected, but when the doctor finally got in there during surgery, it was a *large* mass.

Three other individuals under this doctor's care were experiencing the same symptoms I was, and the tests were not showing that they had heart problems either. What my physician discovered in my situation alerted him to follow through with an echocardiogram on these other three people, to eventually have performed on them the same kind of surgery I had.

So three people's lives that I knew of right then were spared because I went through that surgery. It's no telling how many more lives have been spared since then because I went through what I did.

I believe it has been way too easy for us to look at other people who are going through sickness and disease or who have experienced terrible accidents and to ponder to ourselves, Where is their faith to be healed? Or, What's wrong with them that this was allowed to happen? I've had to wonder if the three individuals who received help because of the heart surgery I endured were perhaps not in a place to exercise faith for their healing. Perhaps they didn't even know to believe God for a miracle, let alone how to believe. Perhaps they weren't even saved, or it simply wasn't their time to go, and so God used me to cause them to get an operation so that they could be spared more time on Earth and even get saved at a later date. And how many others, because of the surgery I endured, might have been and continue to be spared to live a little longer because it hasn't been their time to go or so they, too, can come to know Jesus as Savior and Lord of their life?

Even more could be said along these lines. I know all this might not fit in with some people's theology, but this is how I see the situation. "You're going to come through this victorious," my Father had told me, "but there are two people who need to see you come through this."

For the person who has a hard time believing that God told me this— that there is some kind of theological soundness to what I have just shared— permit me to share a real-life story that might make what I have said a little more palatable. It actually involves the sister of a friend of mine, and the story goes like this.

Pam was coming home from work early one morning after having worked all night in the coalmines on the midnight or "hoot owl" shift. Yes, Pam was one of the first women to go down into the coalmines. Rather than go straight home, which was an hour closer, Pam decided to drive the extra hour and stay at her brother's. This was to soon appear not to have been the best decision.

Tired and not as alert as she would have been had she not worked through the night, Pam headed up the winding West Virginia Turnpike, only to end up in a collision with another vehicle—an accident that was her fault and that sent the driver of the other vehicle to the hospital.

Pam made it on in to her brother's later that morning, and the next day she attempted to drive her damaged vehicle back to her home. Because of the damages to her car—a messed up front left fender—she was unable to go by way of the four-lane turnpike and had to resort to taking a back road and going at a much slower speed. It was a hot day, and she drove with the window rolled down.

At one point along the way, she heard the faint sound of someone crying, "Oh, God! Oh, God! Somebody help me!"

Slowing the car down even more, Pam detected that the cry was coming from over the bank to her left. Stopping the car, she proceeded to investigate, only to find a wrecked pick-up truck, turned upside down, in the West Virginia creek that flowed at the bottom of that bank. A very heavy-set man, reeking of the smell of alcohol, had been partially thrown from the cab of the truck through the back window, leaving his body arched over the top edge of the window's metal frame and completely submerged in the water, with the exception of his head—which he was barely managing to hold out of the water to keep from drowning.

Pam was able to climb under the truck bed only because its tailgate had been thrown about a hundred feet down the creek as a result of the accident. She noticed that the ignition switch of the truck was still turned on and the smell of gasoline was strong; but rather than try to work her way to the switch, she needed to focus on getting underneath this man's bloody body and holding his head out of the water while yelling for help herself. Help came, and the man's life was saved.

When Pam checked on the results of the woman she had sent to the hospital the day before due to the accident that she had caused, the woman told her that because she had gone to the hospital the doctors discovered that she had a blockage in an artery in her neck. This woman continued to inform Pam that had she not had that accident that sent her to the hospital she probably would have died—the doctor at the hospital had told her that she basically had been living on borrowed time.

Now let's look at this picture. Here's Pam driving slowly down a back road, a secondary road, with all its mountainous twisting and turning, when she so much would rather have been batting it down the four-lane turnpike that had cut through the mountains instead of following their winding curves. Inconvenient. And here she is at the wheel of a damaged vehicle—damaged because of an accident that *she* caused—as its front left fender screeches and grinds. Embarrassing. And someone is in the hospital because of the accident that *Pam* caused.

It's one thing for someone else to be at fault when something goes wrong, but when we're at fault, it throws us into such guilt and condemnation and soul-searching, especially in the area of what does this say about what God thinks of us, because His opinion of us—the believer, in particular—matters most of all. And religion, with its emphasis on our having to earn God's love and approval, prompts us to look to our circumstances to determine how God feels about us. If the circumstances are bad and unfavorable, God must be mad at us. If they are favorable, that's a sign that He loves us. We get on this roller coaster of daisy-petal Christianity—He loves me. He loves me not.[3]

So, what about this picture, especially considering that Pam is a Christian, a born-again believer? She loves God with a passion, is in the Word daily, and gives herself to prayer—and she certainly gives financially to the work of the Lord. Where is God in this picture? The conclusion of most people would probably be: someone messed up and missed God.

Granted, God doesn't go around causing accidents and handing out sickness and disease. James 1:17 tells us, "Every good and perfect gift is from above." Though God was going to use my heart surgery to help others, He didn't give me that heart condition. My heart had reached its damaged state no doubt from an accumulation of things, including accidents caused by others. Because we are not islands in this world and are connected to others, we can suffer from our own sins, foolishness, and ignorance and from that of others as well. But God, if we will cooperate with Him, has a way of taking our hardships and sufferings and redeeming them for something good. Even when we have opened the door for something bad to happen, we can appeal to God's mercy and grace and see even those things used for the good. God heard all my prayers concerning my heart condition; He had simply let me know that my road to recovery would be by way of surgery—and for a good reason.

God doesn't go around causing accidents and handing out sickness and disease. But, even at that, we must be careful in drawing our conclusions about what is going on in a seemingly bad situation. What we perceive to be taking place is not necessarily what is really taking place. What appears to be is not *really* what is—not always. For example, what looks holy can often be deceiving, as in Matthew 23:27 (KJV), when Jesus said, "Woe unto you, scribes and Pharisees, hypocrites! for ye are like unto whited sepulchres, which indeed appear beautiful outward, but are within full of dead men's bones, and of all uncleanness." What looks like victory can sometimes really be a defeat. Jesus spoke of gaining the whole world (which could look like a great victory) but forfeiting our soul (the worst kind of defeat). (See Mark 8:36.) And then, what is victory sometimes only looks like defeat—as in Calvary, which looked like the greatest defeat ever. But a crown of thorns was about to become a crown of victory, and a cross was about to become a throne.

So look at Pam's situation again. If her car hadn't been damaged, she wouldn't have been driving that secondary road, let alone having to drive slowly enough that she would have even heard that faint cry over the bank of a creek. Her original plans had been turned upside down. None of this was convenient or comfortable for her flesh. But the end result was that the lives of two people were saved, literally. One woman's life—had it not been for the accident—would have been cut short. And then that man had another chance at life and even a chance at giving that life to the Lord. And then what about all the other lives that were positively impacted—children, grandchildren, friends, co-workers, employers, etc.—because the lives of those two people weren't cut short? So what looked like disaster was a gift of multiple blessings in disguise.

On the Weather Channel recently, in light of all the flooding that had been going on in the mid-West, a mother and two children, unaware that a bridge had been washed out by flooding waters, drove their vehicle straight into a swollen, furiously reeling river. Ensnared by debris, the car came to a stop, affording the older child the possibility of making it to the river's bank, where she had to climb an electric fence before reaching a house where she phoned for help—right before the phone lines went dead due to the storm.

When help arrived they found a vehicle in the river, but it wasn't that of the mother and two children for whom help was originally called. No one knew this second family was trapped as well. The mother and three children in the second vehicle were rescued, and then rescuers reached the other mother and her child, managing to rescue them only seconds before their car broke loose from the debris and was violently snatched away. Had the first vehicle not gone into the water and the daughter managed to escape and call for help, no one would have known that the second vehicle was in river as well. In the end, all were rescued.

Our God is a big God. And He tells us, "For my thoughts are not your thoughts, neither are your ways my ways...As the heavens are higher than the earth, so are my ways higher than your ways and my thoughts than your thoughts" (Isa. 55:8–9, KJV). Remember, He tells us that He will use foolish things to confound the wise. And remember our discussion about going after the one lost sheep at the risk of losing the other ninety-nine and how that might not make a lot of sense—until you or I are the one lost sheep. What if you were one of those three people who needed the same surgery that I did, or one of the only God knows how many others who would need it even later? Would what I went through to bring the knowledge and understanding of that particular surgery about have made more sense to you then?

PART IX

THE SECRET PLACE

Chapter 33

WAITING FOR THE SON

L YING IN INTENSIVE care in the hospital following surgery, I thought, "Oh, boy, if I could just get back to my secret place, I'd be alright." The "secret place"—a section of the woods near where I live—is a get-away to which I would trek (and still do) after slipping away from whatever it was that I was doing. When I was growing up, the woods were a place for me to get away from all that was going on.

As a little girl, when things were just falling down around me and I felt like nobody loved me, my cocker spaniel Mutt and I had a special place we'd go to in the woods, even if it was raining. I would get under a big tree there, and the rain couldn't penetrate the thick canopy of leaves that would keep me dry. And I'd snuggle up with Mutt and feel oh-so safe. I always felt safe in the woods, and the Secret Place in the woods that I have found during my adult years makes me feel the same.

I have no problem walking out there by myself. People say, "Oh, you don't need to go out in those woods by yourself, but I feel safer there than any other place, because I know that Jesus has walked with me in those woods. He's there with me. And what is it that Scripture says? "He who dwells in the *secret place* of the Most High Shall abide under the shadow of the Almighty" (Ps. 91:1, NKJV, emphasis added).

My secret place is a wonderful place to be. Making a percussive contribution to the forest's orchestra of sounds is the splashing, rushing mountain stream that swiftly runs under the footbridge I cross along my familiar path. And then more akin to the string and wind section of instrumental sounds are the singing and chirping of the birds, the buzzing and humming of insects, and the whistling of the wind as it ripples the sea of leaves in its passing through. I take off my shoes and socks and wade barefooted in the breathtakingly chilly mountain water. And it feels *so* good!

When I sold real estate, adorned in my nice designer suits and heels, I would see one of those inviting, picture-perfect streams, sometimes racing and sometimes meandering along the side of the road. And when I did it didn't take much to get me to stop, make my way down a bank or through a thicket, and take off my high heels. And there in that stream I would enjoy the invigorating, therapeutic sensation of that nipping fluid motion, massaging

131

and rushing over those tired feet of mine. Indeed, "beside quiet waters, he restores my soul" (Ps. 23:2–3). Then I'd put my shoes back on and go sell some more real estate. It's amazing just how much that mountain water actually washed away as it refreshed and energized me. There was and continues to be nothing like it!

People who knew I did this would ask, "You're not a country girl, are you?" since what they saw was someone who wore suits and heels and was sophisticated (mainly trying to act that way).

And I would answer, "Yeah, I'm a country girl. Still got mud between my toes." And now that I am a potter, I have mud between my toes *and* fingers. I get to play in mud all day long. I'm the only person in the world that I know who gets to go and play every day.

But back to the secret place. Along its trail there is a hollowed-out place, tall enough to stand in, underneath a gigantic, jutting rock. There in the winter you can see icicles hanging from the massive rock ceiling—like crystal-prism columns that go all the way to the forest's floor. Add to that the surrounding wonderland scene of evergreens standing out starkly against a fluffy white blanket of snow.

When you go out there in the spring it is thick with rhododendron and mountain laurels in bloom, and the air is permeated by an admixture of earthen and heavenly smells. And the birds are lively with their chirping again.

Then summer brings a mood and atmosphere all its own. The heavy rains of spring are over, and the water doesn't run as swiftly and deeply and noisily but rather ripples lazily along with a lulling, trickling sound like the faint pecking on high-pitched piano keys. This all makes for a peaceful, laid-back ambiance that is enhanced all the more by the fragrant smells of lush foliage, the music of the birds, and the scampering of animal life, the flickering of the sun's light as it manages to peak through the overhead leaves, and the soothing effect of the color green, in all its various summertime hues.

And then there is the season of fall—I believe that is my favorite time to visit the secret place. There is nothing lulling about the crackling and crunching sounds as you walk on the plush carpet of leaves. And laid-back is *not* how you feel as you are awestricken every which way you turn by the brilliant production of the sun's light cascading the leaves, both beneath and overhead—intensifying their colors of gold, orange, crimson, sienna, some still-lingering muted green, and every combination of such. The mixture of color, heightened sound, and crisper air evokes sensations of freedom and even wild abandonment, making you want to breathe deep and let loose, like an artist who dares to fling every color on his palette onto the canvas of life. What a place of inspiration—my secret place!

How very important, even crucial, it is that we indulge ourselves with times of getaway like this. Not everyone has a secret place like mine; I'm sure few do. My secret place, though close to where I live and work, is a place that is sometimes a battle to get to in order to grab those few moments, those stolen moments. But it is always worth the time and effort required.

I am convinced that everyone can have a secret place of some sort, someplace where they can slow down. A minister once said that if the devil can't get you to do bad things, he'll get you busy. He knows that if he does you will lose God in the blurred, fast pace of your dizzying speed.

Michael Yaconelli writes, "Most of us don't come home at night staggering drunk. Instead, we come home staggering tired, worn out, exhausted, and drained because we live too fast….Speeding through life endangers our relationships and our souls."[1] And then one last little thought from him along this line: "Rest is choosing to do nothing when we have too much to do, slowing down when we feel pressure to go faster, stopping instead of starting."[2]

Some days I find myself feeling bogged down with decisions—not really having a bad day but just having a lot of things to which to attend. Employees, suppliers, contract laborers, and so on seem to have a million questions every which way I turn. With things closing in on me I go to the secret place, and sitting down by the clear, cool stream, I immerse my tired feet and defy the pushing and pulling and tugging and closing-in that's been going on, allowing myself the luxury, even joy and fun, of stretching those fatigued feet and wiggling my toes, even chuckling a little as I splash and swoosh, creating swirls and whirls.

And I contemplate the wonder of water and *all* of God's creation as I pause to look around. And I thank Him. It's my way of being still and knowing that He is God. (See Psalm 46:10.) It's my way of saying that "God is our refuge and strength, an ever-present help in trouble. Therefore we will not fear" (Ps. 46:1–2).

There happens to be an eagle's nest in the secret place, not far into the woods at the top of a tall tree. The Bible says that "those who hope in the Lord will renew their strength. They will soar on wings like eagles; they will run and not grow weary, and they will walk and not be faint" (Isa. 40:31). The King James Version says that "they that *wait* upon the Lord shall renew their strength" (emphasis added). Did you know that the eagle *waits* for the sun to come up and heat the earth, which in turn heats the air to create thermals so that he, the eagle, can mount up on that essentially sun-heated air to nearly effortlessly reach great heights? He waits for the sun, like we should wait for the Son!

Col Springer writes this about the eagle:

The eagle waits. All other birds about him flap, their ceaseless efforts and wing beating necessary to gain altitude in the cool desert morning [in my case, it would be "in the cool of the forest morning"]...He [the eagle] remains perched quietly on his rocky citadel, completely aloof and disinterested in the comings and goings of the lesser creatures about him. And still the eagle waits. By midmorning the desert [forest] sun has heated the ground temperature sufficiently to cause the thermal currents to begin to rise...Suddenly, by some inner cue or sign, the magnificent wedge tail eagle spreads its awesome wings and virtually leaps into the air. Effortlessly but powerfully, he flaps once, twice, and then he is seized, engulfed by an unseen hand, the thermals....and he rises. Higher and higher, with just the merest flip of the wings, the giant bird soars...Higher, further, and longer he soars, than any other bird in the sky....When the day ends and all other birds are tired, exhausted by their constant efforts to stay aloft, the eagle glides in for a perfect landing. Although he has soared through the sky for most of the day, he is relaxed, poised and tireless.[3]

Quieting myself and resting a spell in the secret place, I place my hope back in the Lord—just in case I've lost my focus on Him. It's amazing how clear everything becomes that beforehand seemed to be running together and getting twisted and gnarled. And I leave with my strength renewed.

For twenty years I've been going to my special place of escape. And much-needed healing has come to me on those grounds. God meets me there. I am convinced that I have heard the Lord tell me that this place is indeed a gateway—a *spiritual* gateway. And I will tell you what I believe that means.

I believe it's a portal of sorts. There are in the earth places where God has met Earth, where He has kissed it, as in places of righteousness where right things, righteous things have been accomplished. There are places where lands, pieces of land—and it doesn't have to be a large piece of land—are set aside by God because of righteous acts that took place there. They have become special places where God has kissed the Earth, and the land is never the same again.

When that happens, there is something that begins to open up in the spirit realm at that location. The Celtic people refer to this opening up as "a thin place." What has come to exist is a very thin place between the spirit realm and the natural realm. There are places like this in the earth, and I believe my secret place is one of these—a portal.

There is a history here, some kind of glorious history. And when a place like this is found, it just doesn't take a lot of pushing and shoving to pray. There is an instant anointing to pray. There are no obstacles that obstruct the voice of the Lord, and therefore, it's a place where He desires to speak to you. It can be a place where revelation flows—having to do with what took place here before that had to do with the revelatory plan of God. It's a well that can be stirred to release revelations from God, perhaps something that He might want to bring to you as part of the equipment you will need to fulfill your destiny in the earth.

To say that this is a gateway, a place where heaven has kissed the earth, is to say that perhaps this is a special place where God met with a man or a woman or a people. Some gateways are places where revival was birthed in times past.

In saying that God met a man or a woman in what I call my secret place, I'm referring to the fact that God, while omnipresent, can also manifest Himself in time and space. And when His presence comes in that fashion, even the land absorbs it and is never the same. The elements, including the soil, recognize their Creator, somehow have an awareness of Him. It's as if they stand at attention.

When Jesus rode through the streets of Jerusalem and the multitudes hailed Him as King, some of the Pharisees said to Jesus that He should rebuke these disciples. But Jesus answered and said, "I tell you...if they keep quiet, the stones will cry out" (Luke 19:40). Jesus said that even the rocks would cry out and praise. I believe He said they would because they could. Isaiah speaks of "the mountains and hills" bursting into song and the "trees of the field" clapping their hands (Isa. 55:12).

I believe there are special, set-aside places in the earth where for some reason or reasons heaven has kissed the Earth, and in those places even the very elements are in worship because their Creator has been there, has manifested Himself in a special way. These are changed places and the location of a gateway. I believe it is a gateway where the darkness cannot enter. And usually at these places there are angelic beings that are assigned to protect them. They are assigned to protect whatever it was and whoever was involved in what took place on these lands before, and they remain there to this day as guardians. And I believe that has much to do with why I feel so protected there in my secret place. I have sensed the presence of angelic beings there, and *many* times.

I believe that places like my secret place have been made special by whatever encounter with God took place there. Heaven kissed Earth there, and the possibility remains for more things to happen. Whenever there is the presence of the Lord, there is always a future. There's always something down the road. There are always a people to be involved. There's always an encounter that God is planning in His heart.

My secret place and all other places like it are sites of a well that can still be stirred, and angelic beings remain as guardians to accommodate future things God wants to do there. They're there to be ready to assist in these "thin places." I believe what has happened is that I have quieted myself in one of these "thin places"; I have learned to tune into the spirit realm, and especially God's Spirit, there during the many times I visited over twenty years.

During that time I've been changed. I'm not the same as I used to be. Having gone through all the ordeals in life that I have, including multiple death experiences, I believe I have been a perfect candidate for becoming more tuned in to the realm of God's Spirit, for making the long trek all the way out to my secret place, for slowing down long enough to notice that it is a place with a difference, for quieting myself long enough to listen and to hear what God wants to say.

And I guess it's a real good thing that I don't run into others along the path of my secret place for yet another reason—I like to do the Teaberry Shuffle when I get out there. For those who don't know, that's a rapid, energetic dance with distinctive shuffling steps popular back in the '60s. After twenty years of not being able to go up and down stair steps and with even walking being a tremendous labor, trekking out to my secret place is more of a thrill to me than ever.

PART X

SOMETHING TO HOLD ON TO

Chapter 34

THE TIM STORY

BEFORE LEAVING THE hospital and leaving my heart surgery behind, I must share what I call "the Tim story." It actually had its beginning one day while I was in my bathroom at home getting ready to go somewhere. I had the radio turned on in the living room; some Christian talk show was airing. I wasn't particularly listening until a certain segment caught my ear, even seemed to become magnified in volume. It had to do with the tendency to compare our earthly father to our heavenly Father.

I remember entertaining the thought, "Lord, I sure am glad that You're not like my earthly father, because it seemed that I could never do enough to please him."

I have already shared that my father was given to drinking after Mother died when I was nine years old. And I've shared all that Dad was faced with when Mother died—being probably no more than twenty-nine himself at the time and having two children to take care of and a house to run that he had left completely up to Mother all the years before, including caring for the yard and garden.

I don't want to be too hard on Dad at this point, but, you know, I could just *never* seem to please him because I couldn't take up the slack where Mother left off. I couldn't cook as well as she did, and I couldn't iron as well as she did. I couldn't do all the things that she did—like can the food, which helped make up the difference for what we didn't have to pay for groceries.

But I was thinking while listening to that radio segment, "I'm so glad, Lord, that You're not like my earthly father. And You're not that hard to please. I don't have to do anything to please You; You just love me anyway."

I thought some more, halfway to myself and halfway to the Lord, "You know, there never was a time that I knew that my dad really loved me."

Immediately, a vision began to appear. I can't say it was out in front of me like some people have visions, but it was more than mere thoughts. It was like a video playback of something that had taken place years and years before. I saw this regular-sized, mahogany bed with a bookcase headboard, and a little girl was lying there with a teddy bear by her side. This teddy bear had a plastic nose and was wearing mittens. The mittens were especially significant in this vision, being that you don't usually see them on a teddy bear.

In the vision, I was aware that this little girl's daddy had won this teddy bear for her at the fair. She named it Tim and placed it by her side *every* night—Tim was her companion. And while this small one was lying there in the middle of her bed, this big, tall, lanky man walked into the room. And, looking down at her, he picked up her bear, raised it up in front of his face, and said, in the gruffest voice he could muster, "Good night, Valinda."

That was the little girl's daddy, who next put Tim back by his daughter's side and gave her a kiss. And I could almost *feel* that kiss on my forehead as that vision unfurled. Tucking daughter and teddy bear in for the night, the daddy endearingly said, "Good night, Valinda. I love you." And he turned to walk out of the room.

I remember thinking right then, "That was so out of character, kissing me and telling me, 'Good night, Valinda.' That was so much out of character for my daddy."

And when the little girl afterward snuggled and came to rest under her layers of covers, I myself felt so cuddly and warm and secure. While I was *seeing* this in this vision, I was *experiencing* it, as well—because I was that little girl, and that was my daddy.

With the vision over, I fell to my knees on the bathroom floor. I mean, I literally fell to my knees as my heart cried out, "Thank you, God! There was a time when my daddy really loved me. I had forgotten. I didn't know. Thank you, God!"

Somehow I had forgotten this about my daddy. It wasn't in my memory. But that day, beholding that vision, I came to realize that my daddy had at one time showed me that kind of love—that he had really loved me. I guess I was forty-five years old when this vision took place, and God had brought back to my remembrance something that had been erased. He did it by allowing me to see a clip of my past like watching a video. I cried from my innermost being that day, "Thank You, Lord! Thank You, Lord! My daddy really loved me!"

As for Tim, I remembered Tim quite well. I will always remember Tim. I could draw you a picture today of what he looked like. What happened is that my aunt came to live with us for a time after Mother died, and she made me put Tim away in the crawl space under the floor. She forbade me to get him out because she said I was too big for teddy bears. But I loved Tim and really needed him, especially at that time. He was my comfort. But she made me put him under the floor of the house, and, of course, he decayed.

My teddy bear rotted, much like any awareness that I had once had of my daddy loving me. I was seeing happen that day what the prophet Isaiah said would happen as a result of the Spirit of God moving upon God's people— "old ruins" and "former desolations" and "the desolations of many generations" would be built and repaired (Isa. 61:4, NKJV). God is in the business of repairing and restoring damage done in our pasts, and especially within our families.

I fell to my knees in the bathroom that day and thanked God for letting me know that my dad loved me, for letting me know that there was a time when my dad *really* loved me. And then God spoke to me audibly. The Lord actually spoke to me in an audible voice, and He said, "Valinda, now *I'm* standing behind Tim for you," referring to taking my daddy's place in that vision where my daddy was holding Tim up before him. And to think that the God of the universe would stand behind a stuffed animal for someone just to let that person know that He loves him or her—that's just how much love He has for His created beings! I know it sounds unbelievable that He would tell me that He was doing that for me, but it happened to me as sure as I'm sharing this with you in this book

My heavenly Father said, "Now I'm standing behind Tim for you."

But there is more to the Tim story, and it has to do with my grandparents on my mom's side. Grandmaw was always cooking a big ol' pan of biscuits, which she would plop down on this big ol' table, spilling some of the biscuits out onto the table top. And along with this she'd put out a good-sized bowl of fresh-churned butter. Grandpaw, who would always sit at the head of the table that seated about twelve people or more, then had the job of buttering those biscuits.

Those sitting around the table would hold up their fingers to show how many buttered biscuits they wanted—one, two, or three. And Grandpaw, after buttering those biscuits, would shuffle them out like shuffling cards. He just threw them to the various plates, and I never saw him miss. That was such a fond memory—Grandpaw shuffling those biscuits out, always hot and buttered with that good country butter, and never missing a plate.

Now, Grandpaw was my hero. I followed him around like a puppy dog, tromping through mud and barnyard poop as he taught me all about the farm. He helped teach my boys to fish and hunt, and I just loved him.

He was an old rascal of sorts who liked big women, with my grandmother being pretty broad. He'd measure how big a woman was by using an axe handle—by measuring how many axe handles wide she was. He always called me "Sis," and if he saw me losing weight, he'd say, "Sis, you just fallin' away to nothin'!" He took notice of women, and if they weren't kind of broad he thought they were sickly-looking. He was quite a character.

Skipping a few decades, I was in the hospital having some tests run on my heart—some of the preliminary work that led to the major heart surgery I previously described. My husband later told me that while I was in the hospital for these tests the Lord gave him an idea—something he was supposed to do for me.

The end result was that he brought me a package, this little teddy bear, one that looked as close as he could get to the Tim I had described to him in times past. The real Tim was a much longer bear, gold and brown, with a plastic nose, and wore little mittens with thumbs. But this was as close as my husband could get to finding a bear that looked like Tim.

And, along with the bear, Bill gave me this letter. It was titled "A Message From Heaven" and was written like it was coming from my Grandpaw, who I so dearly loved. Bill said that when he sat down to write this letter, it just flowed—like it was almost out of his control. Mentioned in the letter are my grandfather, two grandmothers, and Mother and Dad—all of whom passed away years ago and are in heaven now. And this is what the letter said:

A Message From Heaven

Sis, we have been apart for awhile; but this is to let you know we have all been watching over you and are proud of you and what you have become.

Sis, you are falling away to nothing! I wish I could throw you a butter biscuit, but I can't from here, so we got a special friend to give you a special gift from all of us.

When you were young, you had a special friend named Tim. You loved him, and we thought you might like to have him back, so our friend found him for us.

When you go to the hospital, if you need to cough, hug Tim, and he will ease the pain, for we all have put our heart and love in him for you.

—From Grandpaw, both Grandmaws, Mom, and Dad
Be blessed, Love from all of us

I now take this little bear everywhere I go. It was with me in intensive care. After heart surgery, pulmonary infection and even pneumonia are possibilities, and coughing can actually be part of the body's way of dealing with these. But after heart surgery you have an incision where your chest has been split open, so it is important to clutch a pillow to help prevent your chest from expanding during the coughing. The hospital gives you a red, heart-shaped pillow for this very purpose. But, when I coughed, I clutched my new Tim and held onto him.

And to this very day, I place Tim under the part of the seatbelt of my car that crosses my neck, shoulder, and chest to keep it from rubbing me and causing pain. When this causes people to give me a funny look I look back at them and say, "I'm teaching him to drive." I also feel like the Lord has given Tim to me to have something I can hold on to that represents Him.

All kinds of things can be special gifts from God—from real, live pets to stuffed animals—as reminders of His love and presence. It's not that we have to have these; they are not idols. Tim is not real. He's not living; just a piece of fabric with some stuffing. But he is something that I can hold and feel and touch and that represents something very real to me—the love of God. He's just a little piece of God that He gives me to hold on to. He is a special gift.

I've always said, "God is whatever we need Him to be." You hear people describe Him and their experiences with Him, even those out-of-body experiences of going to heaven, and these descriptions and experiences can be very different, because God becomes to them what they need Him to be.

We have to look no farther than the four Gospels to see how He does this. To Matthew, the tax collector, who worked with calculations and had to have things *add up*, Jesus revealed Himself as the one for whom all the prophecies about the coming Messiah *added up*. We see this five times alone in Matthew 1 and 2 as Matthew expressed "that it might be fulfilled" or "then was fulfilled."

To Mark, who was more interested in getting down to business and seeing miracles happen, as is revealed by his oft-repeated expression "straightway" (KJV), we see how Jesus particularly revealed Himself as the Miracle-worker.

To Luke, the physician, Jesus revealed Himself as the Healer of minds, hearts, bodies, and souls—from lepers to the man who fell among thieves to the one lost sheep to the prodigal son who was received back home.

And to John, the beloved, Jesus revealed Himself as the one who "*so loved the world*" (John 3:16, emphasis added).

God was the Husband to the widow in Isaiah 54:4–5 and the Father to the fatherless in Psalm 68:5.

I reiterate: God becomes to people what they *need* Him to be. Now, I'm not saying that what they think they need is what they really need. We discussed this earlier in my story. But God will become to them what they *need*, and He will work with them accordingly.

God knows us to the tiniest detail—even to the number of hairs on our head (Matt. 10:30). We are told in Hebrews 4:13 that "nothing in all creation is hidden from God's sight. Everything is uncovered and laid bare." With this being said, I believe God will deal with us differently for the very same behavior. People are at different places in life, have had different experiences, have had different struggles, and God takes that into consideration.

For example, take two different individuals, women, who are out on the road driving their cars. Each has someone pull out in front of her in traffic, and each has the same reaction—*and it's not a good one.* I believe that God may hold one of these individuals more accountable for her reactions than He does the other. Maybe one of these just went through a horrific time at home, maybe was beaten by her spouse, maybe just had one of her children hauled off to prison for drugs and is devastated and broken-hearted. I believe God doesn't hold this woman accountable in the same way as He does one whose circumstances are entirely different. He says, for example, that to whom much is given, much will be required. (See Luke 12:48.)

Yes, God knows us to the tiniest detail, and He will deal with us differently, according to what we need and what will work best for us. And sometimes someone just needs something to hold on to—like my teddy bear Tim. That's what they need, and God knows it. Tim has meant so much to me, and therefore, I have given teddy bears to other people. They're hurting; maybe they're alone—and they need something to hold on to.

PART XI

DADDY

Chapter 35

"SHE THROWED THAT CERAMIC ROOSTER AND HIT ME!"

THE VISION GOD gave me of my dad and my teddy bear, Tim, opened up a world of understanding about who my heavenly Father is, but it also gave me understanding and closure in regard to whom my earthly father was. Healing in the area of my worth as my earthly father's daughter was evoked as understanding caused me to embrace and cherish my dad and his memory in a way I couldn't have done before. I was free to celebrate the good times and not allow the bad times to have the final say-so in my relationship with my dad—because my heavenly Father had caused me to look past my dad's faults to see his needs and realize his own worth.

Daddy was a very healthy man, and had never been sick much at all in his life. I don't know that he had ever been to the hospital before he got sick that last year and a half, except for the one time I took him to get his lip sewed up. He had shown up at my house with blood running down his mouth, and I asked, "Dad, what happened to you?"

He said, "That woman!"

I asked, "That woman what?"

And he said, "She throwed that ceramic rooster and hit me in the mouth with it."

"Well," I informed him, "I know you don't want to hear this, but we've got to go to the hospital." His lip was gaped open, and he needed stitches to avoid having a bad scar.

After his emphatic, "No," we argued some, and then off to the hospital we went. My sister Barbara, who was living with me at the time, went with us.

The whole ordeal turned out to be hilarious. When Dad got hurt that night he didn't drive himself somewhere else to get help; he had driven all the way across town to *my* house, like a little kid, you know. He always knew that I would take care of everything—that's just how he was.

So there he was standing in the hospital with blood dripping from his lip. And as he was checking in, he was asked by the lady in charge, "Sir, what happened to you?"

"I cut my lip," he replied.

147

And she asked, "Well, how did you cut your lip?"

There was total silence, and he seemed to sit there forever. She asked again, "Sir, how did you cut your lip?"

Dead silence again.

"Sir," the lady persisted, "how did you cut your lip?"

Again, silence—dead silence for the longest time.

And finally he muttered under his breath, "Bumper of the car."

And she said, "Excuse me, sir?"

"Bumper of the car," he replied again, a little more loudly.

"Excuse me, sir," she inquired again. "You hit your mouth *on the bumper of the car*?"

"Yeah."

Barb and I had been standing close enough to hear everything. And we bent over double, heehawing and laughing, and Dad saw us. And talk about looks that could kill—if Dad's looks could have killed, my sister and I would have fallen over dead for sure. We knew that if he could have gotten his hands on us we would have died. But, as it was, he couldn't there in the hospital.

So, as far as the hospital personnel knew that big six-foot-two-inch guy hit his mouth on the bumper of the car. And they took him on back and sewed him up. He wouldn't let us go with him, and I wondered why!

I said, "Oh, God, Barbara, he's going to kill us when he comes out! We're dead! We'd better run now before he gets out, because he's going to kill us."

He had told me, "I's just sitting there, and she picked up that ceramic rooster and just slung it across the room. I was sitting there watching TV. I wasn't doing nothing."

He had been given Novocain to numb the affected area and was then stitched up. And when he came out, his mouth was swollen out even with his nose. It really wasn't funny, but I couldn't help laughing again; he just looked so funny, like Donald Duck.

Once the three of us were back in the car he gruffly asked, "What are you laughing about?"

"I'm sorry, Daddy. I'm sorry. I'm sorry, Daddy," I said. With Barbara having crawled into the back seat, I ended up driving and was situated within slapping distance of Dad's hand. And I had seen that backhand of his, and close enough to count the hairs on it, way too many times. I was within slapping distance, and I just knew Dad was going to knock out all my teeth.

"Daddy, I'm so sorry. I don't mean to laugh, but, uh, I just got to know how in the world did you...I know you had to tell that woman something, and you didn't want to tell her that some woman busted your mouth with a ceramic rooster, but how in the world did you come up with busting your mouth on the bumper of a car?"

And he huffily replied, "Well, you goofball, I could always been pushin' it and slipped and fell."

That was his favorite thing to call me—goofball. "Goofball, goofball!" And though I really thought he would kill me I just could not help but laugh.

Now, Daddy was a truck driver. He delivered meat around a tri-state area. And I advised him, "Well, Daddy, I don't want to tell you what to do or nothing, but I know you don't want to go to work tomorrow and tell those people that a woman hit you with a ceramic rooster. So I think you need to come up with a better story than the bumper of the car."

And I added, "I don't think they're going to buy it. I think I probably would just say, 'That woman done it.' They won't believe you, and they'll just say, 'Yeah! Yeah!'"

And he stated in no uncertain terms, "I'm *not* going to tell them that she—"

I interrupted, "Yeah, but they won't believe you if you say that woman did it. They'll just think it's funny if you say, 'That woman hit me over the head or something. That woman threw something at me.'"

"Just go ahead," I continued, "and tell them that, and they won't believe you. They'll just think you're joking. That sounds a whole lot better than 'the bumper of the car'; I don't think they're going to buy that. That isn't very believable, and I know you want to save face."

And later he told me what happened when he went back to work. "You know what happened? First stop I made, 'Hey, man, what happened to you?' And before I could even say, the fellow said, 'Well, I know, I know! That woman, your stove wood, right?' And I said, 'Yeah, that's what happened. That woman, my stove wood.'"

And he told me he used that explanation the rest of the day. But, looking back, I still find it hard to believe that he didn't just kill me for laughing at him through it all.

Chapter 36

SOME KIND OF PEACE BETWEEN US

THEN DADDY GOT sick with cancer. It was a sudden thing. He had multiple myeloma; that's a kind of leukemia that gets all over you. Even at that we thought right up to the end that he would make it, because he was otherwise such a strong, healthy man. He was just fifty-seven years old when he died and went from two hundred fifteen pounds down to just nothing in no time.

Daddy had been working for his retirement. His plans were to get himself a motor home, get his boat ready, and go fishing. That was all he could think about. And that's all he cared about—retiring so he could go fishing. I was so devastated when this happened to him.

After all those years of me never being able to do anything to please him, now that Daddy was dying of cancer it was funny how the one he really wanted with him now was me—though even in times before, like I've already shared, when he knew he was in trouble I was the one he felt like he could count on.

I had three businesses at the time, and every time I would have to leave my businesses I would have to hire someone to take my place so that I could stay there at the hospital with Dad. I had to be there with him. His wife would be there some, but she had to keep working her shifts to keep up their insurance. And my sister did her fair share. She had to leave her work to spend time with Dad as well. But above all else, Dad wanted me there with him.

What really matters to me here is that Dad and I finally came to some kind of peace between us. We were talking one day around the time of all of this, and he said, "I'm still mad at you."

"What about, Daddy? What are you mad at me about?"

And he said, "Running off and getting married the way you did."

"Daddy, that's been about twenty years now. You mean you're still mad at me?"

He said, "Yeah, I just didn't like the way you did that."

"Well, while we're on that subject," I noted, "you said some really mean, cruel things to me. We [my husband and I] planned on staying there with you and taking care of Barb, and I was going to take care of you and finish up school. But you were so mean and nasty to me. You told me to get my clothes and get out, and you never wanted to see me again."

"Well, I didn't do no such a thing."

"Oh, yes, Daddy. I won't *ever* forget those words. It broke my heart. I won't *ever* forget those words."

"I didn't say that! I didn't do that!" he declared.

"Yes, Daddy, you did. I didn't want to leave like that, but you gave me no choice."

"I didn't do it. You're just a liar! I didn't say that!"

"Yes, Daddy, you did."

And that was the best truce he and I were able to come to—the only truce we could make. He would never admit he was wrong. He would never admit he had done anything wrong.

I reminded him, "Daddy, there were many times you were mean and cruel to me. I knew you didn't have any money, but you would take me and have me pick out fifty or sixty dollars' worth of stuff for Barbara for Christmas, and you wouldn't give me as much as a card. You wouldn't buy me anything. You never acknowledged me."

And I added, "I would have run myself into the ground to make dinner for you, and it was never right. I could never do anything to please you, Daddy."

"Well, you did so. You's a good cook!"

"You never told me that," I recalled. "Nothing I ever did was good enough for you; I never could please you. You never acknowledged my birthdays or Christmas or anything, and you bought for Barbara and you did for Barbara. You would take her to the store and buy her a big sack full of candy for her to bring home and get all over the floor that I had just cleaned up, but you never bought me any. And I would wash, cook, and clean up the kitchen; and I would ask you to just let Barbara dry the dishes when she was of the age I was when Mother died. But you'd tell me that she didn't need to be doing that—that she was the baby and she needed to play. But what was I, Daddy? What was I?"

"Well, I don't remember such a thing! I didn't do that!"

I said, "Yes, Daddy, you did." And that was the end of it. That one conversation was all that was said about all of that. We never talked about it again.

Chapter 37

THOSE ANGELS!

Afterthat Dad and I got to spend many hours at a time together. One time in particular was at the beginning of the illness that left him only a year and a half to live. I was sitting over in this kind of window seat in the hospital when Dad looked up at me and asked, "Did you see that? Did you see that?"

I said, "No, Daddy, see what?"

And he said, "Those angels! They came right up over my bed and right over you and went out that window. You didn't see them? You didn't see them? They went right up over you."

I don't think Daddy had given his heart to the Lord up to this time, though I know he was saved when he died. He may have gotten saved then on that day; I don't rightly know, because at that time I didn't know the Lord well enough myself, not even well enough to win my daddy to Him. I knew there was a God, but I still thought of Him as being that big God *out there*.

There had been a time, a short period of time right after Mother died, that Dad did try to take Barbara and me to a little church. He really did try to go to church right after Mother died, but that didn't last too long.

But he did see angels that day in the hospital. I know he saw them. He wasn't one to be caught up in religious things. He wouldn't be one to fabricate something like that. And Dad wasn't delusional or in any kind of diminished state at that time, having come into the hospital to simply get some blood work done. We were actually just finding out what was wrong with him. He was, in days and months ahead, to become critically ill and go on dialysis. But this was a great day for Dad compared to those days to come.

From the look I saw on his face that day there was no doubt about it that he saw those angels. He sat right up in the bed and asked me, "And you didn't see them? They were right there, and you didn't see them? They went right over your head. You didn't see them?"

152

Chapter 38

FISHING ONE MORE TIME

As it happened, Daddy, though in a considerably weakened state, wanted to go fishing one more time, so Bill and I got out Daddy's boat and took him to the lake. Equipped with minnows and everything else we would need, our trio climbed into the boat, with me being placed in the middle. I actually was the real fisherman of the three, and I hate to fish in the middle of the boat because you can't cast. But I let the guys have the ends. And we were fishing for crappie, though I prefer fishing for bass.

Knowing that we were going to do this with Daddy, I had asked my husband to put out the minnow trap so I could catch some big chub minnows. I like to fish with these. And so, on this fishing outing with Daddy the guys were fishing for crappie with floats and little silver minnows, but I baited my hook with a big chub minnow, added a big sinker to my line, floated it out there, and pulled my line up a little bit so that the sinker would go down to the bottom and my minnow would swim a couple of feet up. That's how I like to fish.

And Daddy said, "Ah, you ain't going to catch nothing with that big ol' thing. Put you one of these little minnows on there and put a float on there and put it up six foot so you can catch something."

Well, neither Bill nor Daddy was catching anything, and they were both fishing just alike. But my line was out there on the bottom without a float, when all of a sudden my pole just bent right down over the side of the boat.

Daddy said, "Ah, now you've got yourself hung up."

I came back with a nonchalant, "Well, maybe so," and let it go at that.

My husband added, "Well, J. C., if she's hung, it's pulling back."

And I wasn't saying a word. I just started *reeling* it in, *reeling* it in, and *reeling* it in. Whatever was at the other end just kept pulling my pole down over the side of the boat. And I would reel in my line a little more. Whatever I had hooked wasn't giving up without a fight. And I continued to pull it in, until up out of the water came the biggest crappie I have ever seen in my life. It was as big as a bass. This was the grandcrappie of grandcrappies. It was trophy material.

I just methodically reached for the creel, plopped that crappie in there, didn't say a word, baited my hook with another big chub minnow, and cast my line back out onto the same spot. After sitting there a minute, once more my rod doubled over the side of the boat—*wham;* and Daddy confidently said, "Now I know you're hung this time!"

"Well, maybe so." And my pole arched down over the side of the boat again, and I pulled it back up again; and it bent over again.

Daddy remarked again, "You bound to be hung."

"Well, maybe so; seems like it's pulling back though." My pole was slamming down the side of the boat again, and I was doing all I could do to pull it back up. And I reeled in whatever was pulling on my line, *reeled* it in, and *reeled* it in; and it was just about the same identical size as the crappie I had just caught. Another trophy crappie!

Neither my husband nor Daddy got even a bite that day. But I got that last fish by the mouth—this one I just had to show off a little. I held it up by its mouth and took a moment to eyeball it, letting it flop a bit; and then I put it over into the creel. And as the guys sat there and fished a little more, Daddy started to squirm. And he squirmed and squirmed. I thought he was going to wear the seat out. And then he managed to say, "Uh, uh, uh, how about letting me try one of them big minners! Let me try one of them ole chub minners."

Bill and I just laughed and laughed and laughed—out of Dad's presence, of course. A simple story I know, but a time with my daddy that was priceless. Still laughing about it, Bill said to me, "Buddy, that took all he could do to ask for one of those minnows."

I saw my daddy's tough exterior right down to the end.

Chapter 39

EVERY SITUATION BUT ONE

HAVING GOTTEN THIS far in the reading of this book, you must have figured out by now that I've seemingly been in almost every situation that you could imagine—or, at least, more than most people you probably know. Remember the beginning of this book? My life is kind of like those superstores where you can buy your groceries, clothing, household goods, tools, gardening plants and supplies, cosmetics, sports equipment, sewing supplies, get your prescriptions filled, stop in to have your hair done, and then get your oil changed while you're doing it all. I'm a one-stop-shopping, able-to-comfort-you-with-the-comfort-wherewith-I-have-been-comforted kind of person.

One situation, however, that I never experienced and wish that I had was to have had parents that lived to a ripe, old age—*elderly* parents that I could have shown love and care during that phase of their life, on that end of their journey. Both of my parents died young—my mother was twenty-seven, and my dad was fifty-seven.

And so it bothers me when I hear people say in a complaining way, "Oh, I've got to go take Mama to the doctor. She's just not feeling good. I get so tired having to do things for her. I just get so tired."

I just want to shake these people and say, "Oh, just be so grateful you have your mom or your dad, or both! Just be so grateful!"

Not everyone knows what it is like to grow up without one or both parents. And, yes, parents can get grouchy in their old age, and they don't do everything like their kids think they should. But the moms gave birth to their children, and I would say that the majority of them nurtured their children. And dads and moms should be shown respect and loved back.

I know that the hustle and bustle and challenges of work and raising our own families can result in weariness and fatigue, and taking care of elderly parents can sometimes seem to be the straw that puts us on overload and breaks the camel's back. But I simply want to encourage those with elderly parents to slow down enough to cherish rather than merely endure their time with them.

I want to encourage those with elderly parents even to record those little sayings that their parents say, those crazy little sayings they've said for as long as the children can remember, because after the parents are gone just about anything would be given to hear their voice and to hear them say those things one more time. In real life you might have gotten sick of hearing some of those expressions, and you might even have thought, "If I have to hear that one more time..." But then, after they're gone, you think, "If only I could hear them say that just one more time. I'd give anything for it!"

I want to encourage those with elderly parents to acquire Mama's recipes, because Mama, most of the time, has them in her head. Take time to make her write them down or either write them down yourselves.

This is the message that I would like to pass onto those who still have their parents with them: Cherish them. Love them. Love them with the love of God. Don't just endure them, because they, for the most part, went through a lot for you. Love them back.

PART XII

SOMETHING IS MISSING

Chapter 40

I'VE GOT TO KNOW FOR MYSELF

A T THE TIME Daddy was dying, I really didn't know how to lead him to the Lord. I had been professing to be born-again for years but can't say for sure that I was. I shared earlier that it was many years later, after I became an adult, that I went back to the same church I supposedly got saved in when I was only nine, and it was then that I was pointed to God in a tremendously impacting way.

A big revival was going on, and a guest preacher was scheduled to minister. I was hearing that everybody was being slain in the Spirit, which, for those who don't know what this means, is an experience whereby the presence of God is so strong that the individual falls backward, to remain in the Lord's presence for a duration of time. And I thought, "Well, I need to go back down there. There's something missing in my life. There's something missing, and I need to go back and figure out what it is. Something isn't right in my life."

So I went. And as the guest preacher would reach forth his hand, everybody on every pew was falling, being slain in the Spirit. He would reach his hand toward them, and everybody was falling out like dominoes in every pew—except when he got to me and two or three others. We didn't fall down.

The minister said, "The ones that didn't go down, come up front. I want to pray for you special."

Well, he prayed for us, and the others who didn't fall down before fell down around me. But I didn't fall. And I remember thinking, "Well, I wonder what's wrong with me. What have I done? What is wrong? Everybody else in the whole church is lying in the floor. What's wrong with me? Oh, God, what is wrong?"

I remember leaving that church that night. I was going to spend the night at my sister's house, and I remember saying to the Lord on my way there, "Lord, You're just going to have to get me home." It was pouring down rain, and the tears were pouring down my face—both so badly that I could hardly see to drive. I was gulping on both the tears and my prayer.

I was an adult, oh, thirty-some, I guess, and I was crying out, "Lord, there's more than meets the eye. There's more than meets the eye here, and I want to know about this. Either all these folk are wrong, or I am."

And I pleaded, "You've got to show me what's going on here. I just do not understand this. If whatever they've got is real, then I want it too. And whatever they have that isn't real, let me know that too. I need to know something, and I need to know it *now*. I can't take this anymore. You've just got to tell me something."

I went to my sister's house and let myself in. She and her husband had already gone to bed, and she had a mattress laid out for me on the living room floor. I fell onto the floor and cried, "Lord!"

I was so distraught that I was screaming, though I kept it stifled so as not to be heard by others in the house. I begged, "God, I've got to have some answers here; I can't take this. I want to know. And if I need something else, I want You to give that to me as well. Whatever it is, I've got to have it—*the more*. I know there's *more*, and I want whatever it is."

I had my old Bible. It was just a cheap Bible, but I've still got it—wouldn't take anything for it, wouldn't take *anything* for that Bible. And, I just happened to have a red pen on hand. To my utter amazement, I speed read for the first time in my life. The pages in that Bible were just a-turning. I mean, I was reading them like I had never read before in my life. And that red pen was marking and underlining right and left.

The Scripture that was being brought to my attention was telling me that I was not under the Law; I was under grace. It told me that I was under grace, and I was God's child, that He *loved* me. I underlined, and I underlined. I mean, I went through that whole Bible with that red pen as God told me how much He loved me. That night I was forever changed. I was filled with the Holy Ghost there in my sister's living room, lying on the floor, and I returned to my home to pull out every interpretation of the Bible and every reference book I could get. I shut myself up in my bedroom and came out only long enough to fix something to eat and do whatever else I needed to do.

My husband came into the bedroom and asked, "What in the world are you doing?"

I said, "I'm tired of taking man's word for it. I want to know for myself. I'm reading this Bible, and I am going to read until I understand. And if I don't understand it in one Bible, I'm going to read it in another. I'm going to find out for myself, because I'm tired of taking man's interpretation for it. I've got to know for myself. This one says this, and that one says that. And then this one says that over there."

I continued, "I've got to know for myself! I've asked God to teach me, and He's going to."

Now, like I said, I had all these different translations of the Bible laid out, and my husband half-asked and half-told me, "Well, don't you know that you'll go to hell if you read any kind of interpretation of the Bible besides the King James?"

And I said, "That's *exactly* what I'm talking about. Show me here in this Bible where it says that."

"Well, I don't know where it says it."

And I asked, "Well, how do you know that's true?"

"Well, Brother So-and-So said that."

And I asked, "Well, where did Brother So-and-So get it at?"

"Well, I don't know; that's just what he taught me."

And I said, "Well, until you can show me here in this Bible, I'm not believing it. That's just what I'm talking about. This one says *this*, and that one says *that*; and this one says *that over there*. I don't think my God would allow all these other interpretations of the Bible to be written if He didn't want people to learn."

And I added, "And I'm staying in here until I find out for myself, because I'm sick and tired of taking somebody else's word for it."

I shut myself in for two weeks to find out for myself; and I'm telling you that I learned more in those two weeks than most, I truly believe, learn from the Word of God in a lifetime. I had gotten fed up with where I was spiritually, and I had come to the place of refusing to be held back any longer as a result of not having been brought up in church and not having had anyone teach me much of anything in the Word.

My husband and I had been going to a certain church together at this time. We were members there. But I had felt drawn to go to that church that I was at that night as a nine year old after my mother died. While the people there may not have reached out to me like they should have when I was there about twenty years or so before, they had something I needed. I knew something was missing in my life. There was something missing, and I found it lying on my sister's living room floor after I had visited that church once again. That inexpensive Bible I had that night—and still have—is ripped all to pieces now. I have read it and re-read it and re-read it and re-read it until it's essentially shredded, so I have very carefully and gently put it away for safe-keeping, *never* to part with it.

It was that night that I really came to know the Lord—when He led me to all those verses on grace and the Law. He showed me that I was under grace, not under the Law.

Chapter 41

IT'S A MESSAGE OF GRACE

THE MAIN MESSAGE of the Gospel isn't about sin, judgment, or God's rules. It's not even about righteousness. *Not really.* At least, it isn't about *our* aspiring to righteousness. The devil has no problem with righteousness—as long as he can deceive us into pursuing our *own* righteousness. The devil doesn't even have a problem with us serving God—as long as we are not serving the true God, as long as we see Jesus as only one of many ways to heaven. Of course, that can't be so, because the Bible tells us that He is the *only* way to heaven.

> I am the door. If anyone enters by Me, he will be saved.
> —JOHN 10:9, NKJV

He also says, "Most assuredly, I say to you, he who does not enter the sheepfold by the door, but climbs up some other way, the same is a thief and a robber" (John 10:1, NKJV). So if Jesus were to be only one of many ways to heaven, then He would be a liar, and then, why would we even look to Him as being a Way—period?

The issue of righteousness has been one of the enemy's most valuable weapons. I believe that the greatest deception on the earth today is a church or individual controlled by a religious spirit. Keeping us preoccupied with pursuing our own righteousness keeps us sidetracked and using our time and energies to that end, rather than about the business of bringing God's kingdom into the earth as it is in heaven. We stay busy do-do-doing to get something that is already done, done, done. And then we never receive, receive, receive what a relationship with the God of the universe has to offer.

We have already been made righteous through Jesus's atoning blood. My righteousness does not come from my living holy and doing everything right. When I was born again, I was "created in righteousness and true holiness" (Eph. 4:24, KJV). My new nature was created to be righteous. It's not something I'm becoming or evolving into.

Religion or the religious spirit says to live by what we can accomplish in our own ability. But God delights in us simply because we are His. And nothing, nothing, nothing can separate us from His love—"neither death nor life, neither angels nor demons, neither the present nor the future, nor any powers, neither height nor depth, nor anything else in all creation" (Rom. 8:38–39).

Religion keeps us under the Law, but grace, on the other hand, "'means there is nothing we can do to make God love us more...and there is nothing we can do to make God love us less. God already loves us as much as an infinite God can possibly love'....Our only choice is whether or not to live loved."[1] And I have made that choice—to *live loved* every waking and sleeping hour of my life.

> For it is by grace you have been saved, through faith.
>
> —EPHESIANS 2:8

Chapter 42

GROWING, GROWING, GROWING

I STARTED GROWING AND growing and growing. I actually became very active in this little church my husband and I were then attending, and it was during this time that I was healed of the flesh-eating disease. I returned from the hospital to tell everybody in my church about my experience—about seeing angels and being miraculously healed. And the people, the leadership in particular, were appalled.

"You need to be quiet about that," I was told. "You don't need to be talking about all that!"

And the intern pastor of that church said from the pulpit, "That healing that is talked about in the Bible in Isaiah 53:5 is *spiritual* healing. The healing that comes as a result of Jesus's stripes is *spiritual* healing. And anybody who says they talk to the Lord and they see angels and all that stuff, they just need to talk to me. I've read the Bible so many times, and if God was going to actually speak to anybody, He'd speak to me."

And I said to myself, "Well, hold it a minute!" And I had a meeting with that pastor. "I want to tell you something. I do talk to the Lord, and He talks back." And I said, "I *have* seen angels, and I *have been* miraculously healed. And you can't dispute that!"

And I asked him, "If 'by His stripes we are healed' in Isaiah 53:5 (NKJV) only refers to *spiritual* healing and not physical healing, then why did Jesus have to take those physical stripes on His back? They were going to kill Him anyway; they were going to hand Him over to the cross and kill Him anyway. So why did He have to take those physical stripes? He died for our sins, but why did He have to take the beating, also? Was that for our *spiritual* healing, as well?"

"Yes," was the reply, "that was for our *spiritual* healing." And then this pastor let me know again that I needed to be quiet about all of this, adding to his argument that Sister So-and-So in the church was a very devout Christian, and she hadn't been healed. His point was that it would make her feel bad because she was such a good Christian and she didn't get healed while I did (though he didn't really believe that healing was for today). I just didn't get the meaning of that.

I responded, "Well, what am I, 'chopped liver'? I can't help it because God miraculously healed me, and I'm *not* going to be quiet about it. I'm going to shout it from the rooftop!"

I know I was stirring things that this pastor didn't want stirred. He didn't have answers for this other lady. He didn't even have his own answers—not really. He didn't want me drawing this lady's attention to the fact that Jesus does heal and, therefore, stirring things.

And I further stated to that pastor, "Because God is *still* in the miracle business, and He performed a miracle on me, if you think I'm going to sit down and keep my mouth shut about God still performing miracles today, you're sadly mistaken."

"Well, women are not supposed to speak out in church!" I was told.

And I asked, "Where do you read that?"

I got really bold after the Lord set me free. I got *really* bold. And I couldn't stay in that little church anymore after they told me I had to be quiet about my Lord and after they got up there telling lies about Him—that He wasn't healing today. I mean, both of those are lies: that I had to be quiet and that Jesus wasn't healing today. I couldn't stay there anymore. And what times I did attend before I left, it was like sitting on a chair of firecrackers, because I just wanted to pop up and say, "How dare you all say that about my Lord! How can you do that?" I came to figure that the best thing for me to do was not stay there rather than interrupt the service—because I would never do that.

I had outgrown what they were teaching me there. This is not to say that they had *nothing* to offer me or that I didn't need anything they had anymore. But they didn't have it all. And I wanted the all of God's Word and plan for my life.

I stopped going to that church, and while I have and continue to attend other churches and firmly believe in the assembling of ourselves together in the body of Christ, I have my pottery business open seven days a week—and I am truly ministering there. The Lord has told me that this is where I am supposed to be, and I believe Him. Like I stated earlier, Miracle Pottery is essentially not a business but a ministry.

Chapter 43

HIS IDEAL OR YOURS?

To give an example of how we can get hung up on what we consider to be ideal and completely miss God's ideal or conception of what something should look like or how it should be done, I will share something else that happened at this little church I had been attending when God healed me of the flesh-eating disease. It had come time to add onto the church. The fellowship hall was not big enough to hold the congregation because the church was growing, so we built a new one.

Well, the first Sunday we were in it, it was too small. It couldn't hold all the people. And because I used to be in the building business, I kept saying during the building of this fellowship hall, "We're not building this *big* enough."

"Well, we're building it according to our plans that we had drawn up," I was told.

I asked, "Are your plans *big* enough?"

And they said, "Well, we've already got it drawn up this way."

And I asked again, "But do you not need to rethink it and make it bigger? Our church has grown since you made the plans."

"Well, it's already on the diagram, and we've already voted it in. And blah blah blah."

And I said, "OK. Alright. You know, y'all go with it."

The fellowship hall was built, and the first Sunday we used it, it was too small. It didn't hold the people. But phase two of this building plan to accommodate our growing congregation had yet to be implemented: we were going to build extra Sunday school rooms. We, naturally, were outgrowing the Sunday school rooms along with the fellowship hall that we had already replaced.

But the plan was to build a bunch of *little* rooms. And my way of looking at it was that the Sunday school program didn't need more *little* rooms; we needed *larger* rooms to accommodate the size of the classes. The rooms in the plans weren't any larger than the ones we already had. There were just *more* of them. The direction we were going was not going to benefit us, so I expressed this to those who were in charge.

"Well, this is according to our plans. This is what we had drawn up," was the same ol' song, just like I was told in regard to the recent building of the new fellowship hall.

166

I said, "Well, may I suggest that maybe we take the fellowship hall that we have now that's too small and make Sunday school classes out of that? We could take the sanctuary that we have now that is overrun—we're having to put out folding chairs to make room for everyone—and make that the new fellowship hall. And let's build a new sanctuary!"

"Oh, well, that's not in our plans. We can't do that."

When I asked if they had actually prayed about all of this, not one of them indicated that he had. God was showing me the picture to build a bigger sanctuary, turn what was now the sanctuary into a fellowship hall, and take the fellowship hall that we just built and make it into Sunday school rooms. And I was trying to explain this.

I emphasized, "Guys, you are going in the wrong direction. We're not going to be any better off heading in the direction that we are. You are going to have empty Sunday school rooms."

"Well, this is according to our plans, and we've already voted on it. This is what we're going to do."

They could not tell me that they had prayed about it. Instead, they went on with *their* plans. And guess what? Our attendance went down, down, down to about twenty-five people—from about four hundred people to about twenty-five.

Now, that's what happens when we don't consult God—when we've decided upon what *we* think is ideal, and our idea of ideal isn't God' idea of ideal. That's what happens when we think that because we have a deacon board, we don't need God: "Unless the Lord builds the house, its builders labor in vain" (Ps. 127:1).

God had shown me the vision of what He wanted, but I was just a woman, and in this church women didn't have a voice. I had some business expertise and wisdom in this regard, but women didn't have a voice in this church. It didn't matter if God painted a painting and hung it around her neck—a woman wasn't supposed to have a voice in the church. Period. And especially not in *this* church. So, needless to say, for this and other reasons that I already discussed, I don't attend that church anymore.

PART XIII

TURNING FOR GOOD WHAT
WAS MEANT FOR HARM

Chapter 44

THE LITTLE ONES

THE LORD GAVE me a vision in the night awhile back. Perhaps it was a dream, but it seemed more real to me than that, so I will call it a vision. What matters is what the Lord saw fit to reveal to me at that time. I was making pottery in this vision. I was making pottery—and lots of it—at my potter's wheel. And when I would return to my shop the next day, those pieces of pottery would have the tiniest little footprints embedded in them, just like some little one, a little human being, had walked across them while the clay was still fresh. And then I'd make some more pots, only to go into my pottery shop the next day and find these little footprints once more pressed into certain pottery pieces, like some little someone had walked across each piece before it had time to dry.

And I said to the Lord in this vision, "I don't really understand what this is about."

He responded by reminding me of the time in my life when I had lost a baby—when I went through an abortion. And He reminded me of all the little babies who had gone on before who had never gotten to put their feet down on this earth, who had never gotten to leave even a footprint showing they had been here. He impressed upon me that they wanted to leave their mark somewhere.

Then the Lord made me aware that there were all these hurting moms who had lost little ones due to abortions or miscarriages or whatever other reasons. He called my attention to their having never gotten to see their baby, having never gotten to hold him or her in their arms. This left these moms without some kind of finality or closure, without a sense of their child's earthly time coming to a conclusion *because that child had never had a tangible sort of beginning or presence.* There is no grave to visit, no gravestone bearing the child's name, date of birth, and date of departure. There are no photographs of times shared.

The mother is left to put the connection she had with this little one in the back of her mind or, in some cases, to try to forget about this tiny being altogether. But that little life just doesn't go away. There remains a gaping, unhealed wound. This vision helped me face the reality that I hadn't had closure with my own child and that I needed healing where she was concerned.

And what the Lord was doing was giving me an idea to help myself and multitudes of others receive just this—closure and healing in regard to their little one, closure and healing that they might otherwise not receive.

He showed me, in a beautiful piece of pottery indented with those little footprints, that these mothers could have a keepsake, a memento, that stated in a special way that their child was real, was here, and left a mark. This would be something visible and tangible that bore witness to the mark of that child's presence, which was already very, very real, as it was indelibly imprinted on the heart and mind of the mom who had carried him or her.

The little footprints I saw in that vision were about the size of the feet of a developing fetus—tiny, tiny. And they were imprinted across the most beautiful platters and trays. And as I pondered this vision, I could actually see how these footprints came to be each night when I would leave my shop and leave behind these trays and platters that had been freshly molded at the end of the day.

I could see the little ones showing up in my shop. They were extremely cautious and hesitant at first, initially pressing only their toe onto the wet clay, testing its consistency and possibility—as one would do if he or she was very carefully making the first strokes on the canvas of the one self-portrait to ever be painted, as one would do if he or she was about to make the initial cut into the wood or stone that was to become the one and only sculpture this individual would ever sculpt and be remembered for.

But after that initial pressing of the toe into the moist clay and then a cautious placing of the entire foot onto the pottery's surface, restraint was thrown to the wind, as the joyful and thrilling trek was made to the other side—putting into one brief run from one end of the pottery piece to the other all the excitement and marvel of an entire day spent at Disney. It was sheer abandonment, yet with attention to brevity of time, as these little ones were in a hurry to accomplish their goal before the morning came and the shop was opened for another day. It was a deeply touching sight, beautiful to behold!

I had asked the Lord when He saw fit for me to see these little footprints on my pottery. "Well, what is this? Where are these footprints coming from? I don't understand." And then as I afterward pondered the vision and its meaning was disclosed, I did not only *see* how the footprints came to be, but I *heard* in my spirit the conversation of these little ones as they accomplished their feat: "I can do this. I can make it happen. I just want it to be known that I was here and that it mattered that I was here. I want someone to know that I was here. I was here! I was here!"

And then, by the Spirit of God, I saw myself coming into my shop each day to find more and more and more footprints, as though some kind of gathering was taking place. And then I heard, again in my spirit, "We've found a place to make our mark! Yeah! Come on! Hey, Susan! Come on over here. We found a place to make our mark. Come on. Put your mark over there. And, Charlie, put your mark over here."

The word had gotten out: "There's a place you can go to make your mark." And more and more little ones were called in, and the numbers grew.

For the most part, the world doesn't recognize that these little ones were here, but in that mother's heart, he or she was. That child is still carried in her heart. And this piece of pottery is something visible and tangible from that child that says, "I touched my foot down on this earth. I was real. I was here."

I have available in my shop these pottery pieces—platters, trays, and even bowls—with the footprints of the little ones engraved on each piece. And they have beautiful coats of glaze to enhance their value as a treasured piece of art. And just as each child, each human being, who has ever come to this earth is unique, each one of these pieces of pottery is unique. No two are alike. I've already made mention that Miracle Pottery doesn't make anything with a mold. Everything is fashioned by hand.

I have the story that goes with these footprint pottery pieces in a separate book all its own. There are pictures to see. And those pictures paint thousands of words—words that I foresee as instruments in the hands of the Great Physician to perform surgery on the hearts and souls of wounded mothers worldwide. There is a little one to be touched and embraced in all of this, and that little one, from the pages of that book and a corresponding piece of pottery, will, in turn, touch the mother for whom his or her message is meant. It is a *healing* story. It is a *freeing* story.

And it is a tool—even a weapon—to put into the hands of the person who is contemplating an abortion and trying to convince herself that this that she carries on the inside is an "it" and not a "he" or" she"—in a day when the world argues, after the fetus has been aborted, that a "he" or "she" never existed there. Yet, that is not what God's Word says about that little one, even while it is being fashioned in the mother's womb:

> For you created my inmost being; you knit me together in my mother's womb. I praise you because I am fearfully and wonderfully made; your works are wonderful, I know that full well. My frame was not hidden from you when I was made in the secret place. When I was woven together in the depths of the earth, your eyes saw my unformed body. All the days ordained for me were written in your book before one of them came to be.
>
> —PSALM 139:13–16

I am reminded of when my niece had to have a DNC after she had miscarried her child. Her sister, who had gone to the hospital with her for this procedure, told me that the baby was dismissed by the hospital staff like it was nothing, as though they, the staff, didn't understand that it was her sister's *baby*. With disgust and hurt, she expressed, "That was her baby! We had heard his heart beat, and they dismissed it like it was nothing. And they didn't even console her—*and it was her baby!*"

Chapter 45

DATE RAPE AND ABORTION

As for the baby that I never got to hold, she did have a name. I named her Veronica Lynn. I have no proof that she was a little girl; I could not bring myself to look at her. But somehow I knew in my heart that she was the one little girl I had always wanted, and I had caused her death. I didn't want to name her for a long time. I had pushed what I did—the abortion—so far back in my mind because I couldn't deal with it. Oh, how I couldn't deal with it! It took me sharing about this at three different churches—with God compelling me to do so—before I truly began to face it for what it was in all its ramifications. I didn't want to. I went kicking and screaming every step of the way. And I *never, ever* wanted anybody else to know what I did.

It is still a very painful matter for me, but I share about it now in order to help someone else. When I finally told my two boys about the abortion it hurt them terribly, but they are adults now and want my story to help someone else.

In many respects, I was a baby myself at the time. I had gotten married at fourteen, and by the age of twenty-two I had been married eight years, had two children, and was divorced. The first guy that I dated after I was divorced raped me, and I became pregnant. I was working three jobs. I had decided that if you couldn't pay the bills, you got another job. But even with three jobs I could still barely feed my children. I did not know how I could afford to take time off from work to have this baby, let alone to raise it, when I could barely take care of the two children I had and then my sister as well. She was about six years younger than I and had come to live with me. With all of this going on, there was no way I could take care of another child. That is, *I thought there was no other way!*

I allowed the circumstances surrounding this child's conception—she was the product of a rape—to make it all the more difficult for me to embrace her as my own. I knew that because it was a date rape, "I had obviously asked for it"—you know, that's what people so often think and say! And the aggressor was one of those guys like my former husband in that he was a manipulator who tried to place the blame and guilt on me.

"Well, it's not like you haven't been there before. You've got *two* children!" Those were his coldhearted words that rang in my ears.

The entire ordeal became staggeringly overwhelming, more than I could seemingly bear. No matter how much I cried out, it didn't make any differ-ence—no more than it did when my boys' father brought his girlfriend home and told me he was in love with her. I cried out, confused, shocked, and broken-hearted, only to be told that there wasn't anything I could do about it.

What was I to do? I agonized. If only I had someone to turn to. I consid-ered God but questioned, How could He help me now? I mean, really, after what I had done—gone and gotten myself in a situation like that! So, I turned to an abortion clinic and was assured that "it" wasn't a real baby. "It" was only a mass, and the procedure to remove "it" would be simple. I would be able to swiftly return to work and life as usual, like *nothing* had ever happened.

And nobody knew. I worked on the assembly line building stoves and left work one day at lunch to go to the hospital for this "simple medical proce-dure." Back then I was too far along in the pregnancy to simply go to the clinic. Upon arriving at the hospital I had to remove my clothes and put on a gown. A large needle filled with salt water was inserted into my abdomen and then into my womb. The nurse gave me a call button and instructed me to call her when it was over. I was in the room with three other girls, but we did not talk to each other.

I suffered death in more ways than I could have ever imagined. I went through all the labor pains of having a baby—and all alone—with no pain medication and realizing, as far as I was concerned, that what I had just done was the most horrible thing a person could do.

How I struggled, crying to myself, "What have I done? What have I done? What have I done? God, please forgive me. I killed this baby. I killed this baby. What have I done?"

I had been told that "it" wasn't a *real* life. Then I lay there and birthed that baby. I had already given birth to two babies, and I was now going through all the pains once more of birthing what I knew was *a baby*, not an "it." I died with every pain I felt. I died because I knew I was killing my *child*.

I wanted to stop the abortion, but it was too late. I lay there in tears as my baby died and as I died a thousand deaths. I would never, ever be the same again, and like I've already shared, I knew in my heart that I had caused the death of the one little girl I had always wanted.

I used the call button to instruct the nurse that it was over. I put on my clothes, and when I walked out of that place into what felt like total darkness I was feeling worse than what I figured any murderer on death row would feel. There was no one to whom I could turn. I went home and took a shower but felt like I would never be clean again.

I was back at work at seven o'clock the next day on the assembly line building stoves again, just as if nothing had ever happened. And still nobody knew.

I continued struggling to raise my boys, but the passing of time did not stop the wondering, *How could God forgive me?* It wasn't until I had that encounter with God while lying on my sister's living room floor, where I truly found Jesus as my personal Savior and friend, that I was able to forgive myself. I had asked Jesus's forgiveness, and my sins were covered in His precious blood. Scriptures that have continued to strengthen me are:

> As far as the east is from the west, so far has he removed our transgressions from us.
>
> —PSALM 103:12

> I, even I, am he who blots out your transgressions, for my own sake, and remembers your sins no more.
>
> —ISAIAH 43:25

> I have swept away your offenses like a cloud, your sins like the morning mist. Return to me, for I have redeemed you.
>
> —ISAIAH 44:22

> Surely it was for my benefit that I suffered such anguish. In your love you kept me from the pit of destruction; you have put all my sins behind your back.
>
> —ISAIAH 38:17

> You will again have compassion on us; you will tread our sins underfoot and hurl all our iniquities into the depths of the sea.
>
> —MICAH 7:19

> The blood of Jesus, his Son, purifies us from all sin.
>
> —1 JOHN 1:7

> To him who loves us and has freed us from our sins by his blood.
>
> —REVELATION 1:5

Chapter 46

LETTING GO

QUITE UNDERSTANDABLY, WHAT God had given me to do by way of the "little ones" book and the accompanying footprints pottery was significant beyond words to express. It was His way of turning around for good in my life and possibly in the lives of multitudes of others what had been meant for harm. It was a way for me to give back. It was about restoration, which is at the heart of God's redemptive package.

The book about the little ones and their pottery had come to me in the middle of the night. The Lord gave it *to me*. It wasn't a matter of me wanting my name on the book or the pottery or being given credit for both, as opposed to someone else. It was about something that I knew I was *supposed* to do and *wanted* to do and was *vehemently passionate* about. It was *my* assignment—not someone else's. To follow through with this had something to do with me being in the place of *my* call "according to His purpose" (Rom. 8:28).

After the "little ones" vision in the middle of the night, I had gone to work designing and crafting the "little footprints" pottery. The tiny shape and dimensions of the little footprints came together with precision, and the Lord began to pour into my spirit the contents of the book that was to accompany this.

It was sometime afterward that a certain individual actually attempted to steal my idea—my story—and make it into his own. But the good news is that—whether self-imposed or brought on by others—robbery, affliction, shame, *whatever*, in all their shapes and sizes, do not have the last word on the matter of our destiny. Because we have a Father who loves us unconditionally and who empowers us by the very revelation of that love, we can let go of hurts, wounds, issues, and immaturity and refuse to stay any longer in whatever cesspool we have been in—where we have listened to lies that we are unloved and unlovely, alone and lonely, failures, rejects, castaways, or condemned to a life of grief and despair over poor choices and lost opportunities.

We can let go of grudges and unforgiveness—even *never* entertain these to start with. Because of the love of God, I am able to quickly forgive just as soon as someone, *anyone*, does something to me. And I can do it from my heart and, consequently, take away any ammunition that could cause me further harm that would come from carrying malice and unforgiveness toward anyone. I walk in total freedom in this respect.

I simply do not let things, people included, get to me, get under my skin. Not anymore. I have destroyed any and all paths of bitterness, malice, and unforgiveness, along with the paths of resentment and regret and even shame. I have found security in my Father's love. I have learned to *live* loved.

There is an interesting story shared by the prophet Nehemiah about the Jews who had returned to rebuild the walls of Jerusalem after they had been destroyed years before by the Babylonians.

> When Sanballat [governor of nearby Samaria] heard that we were rebuilding the wall, he became angry and was greatly incensed. He ridiculed the Jews, and in the presence of his associates and the army of Samaria, he said, "What are those feeble Jews doing? Will they restore their wall? Will they offer sacrifices? Will they finish in a day? Can they bring the stones back to life from those heaps of rubble—burned as they are?"
>
> —NEHEMIAH 4:1–2

Sanballat asked, "Can they bring the stones back to life from those heaps of rubble—burned as they are?" And the answer is yes. God does it all the time. He takes and uses for the fulfilling of His purposes the foolish, the weak, the overlooked, the unqualified, the cast aside, and the left for dead—those who have been burned as they have gone through the fire. Quite interestingly, a stone (or brick) that has been fired is stronger than it originally was!

> Noah was a drunk. Abraham was too old. Isaac was a daydreamer. Jacob was a liar. Leah was ugly. Joseph was abused. Moses had a stuttering problem. Gideon was afraid. Samson had long hair and was a womanizer. Rahab was a prostitute. Jeremiah and Timothy were too young. David had an affair and was a murderer. Elijah was suicidal. Isaiah preached naked. Jonah ran from God. Naomi was a widow. Job went bankrupt. Peter denied Christ. The Disciples fell asleep while praying. Martha worried about everything. The Samaritan woman was divorced, more than once. Zaccheus was too small. Paul was too religious. Timothy had an ulcer. AND Lazarus was dead![1]

PART XIV

OUR PURPOSE

Chapter 47

A PICTURE THAT PAINTS A THOUSAND WORDS

I CONSIDER MY VERY life to be a painting of sorts—a picture that paints a thousand words, one that will hopefully cut to the chase and help someone or several someones be better positioned to live their lives more abundantly, successfully, and zestfully because of what they have learned from mine. My life may seemingly have had more than its fair share of tragedies—of trouble, perplexing times, persecutions, and being cast down, but ultimately, because of Jesus and even in spite of my own moments of giving in to distress and despair, I was not forsaken nor destroyed. (See 2 Corinthians 4:8–9.)

I've done my share of bleeding, *but I am alive!* Remember, it's dead skin that doesn't bleed! I seem to have found myself on more than one sinking ship, but because of God's love and mercy I didn't drown. I rather consider myself to be like one of those in the movie *The Titanic* who was on the lifeboat pulling others out of the frigid North Atlantic waters—and *not* like one of those who rowed as fast and far away as she could from the pleas and cries of the drowning mass, forgetting the horror she herself had felt before a lifeboat came her way. God has comforted and revealed Himself to me miraculously, delivering me out of all my troubles, and, therefore, I am now able to "comfort those in any trouble with the comfort [I] have received from God" (2 Cor. 1:4).

And God has blessed me to be able to do this in numerous ways, in different venues, using various means. And actual painting has been one of these means whereby I can comfort others with the knowledge and understanding that there is an all-knowing, all-loving, all-capable, miracle-working God in our midst.

God transformed my inability to draw even a half-decent stick man into something that in His hands would produce near life-size oil paintings that grace the homes of multitudes. And just as miraculous as this was for someone who once believed she had no artistic ability whatsoever, each of my paintings have to do with the miraculous.

"Turning Water to Wine."

"Turning Water to Wine"

I was awakened in the night and given a vision of my first painting—
"Turning Water to Wine." Of course, Jesus's turning water into wine at the
marriage in Cana in John chapter 2 was His very first miracle recorded in the
Bible. Scripture tells us that He "kept the good wine until now" (v. 1, KJV), or,
as it is often translated, "He saved the best wine for last."

When God gave me the vision of what this first painting was supposed to
look like I scrambled through my nightstand drawer to find pen and paper to
sketch what I had seen. The next morning He spoke to me and said, "Valinda,
I want you to paint this."

Up to that point I had taken no more than two one-day painting courses
and had been doing some *little* paintings, but never had I undertaken something of the magnitude I was about to do. Seemingly strapped by what was
turning into a long and difficult time of recuperating from the flesh-eating
disease, I had time on my hands.

The Lord gave me a picture in the vision of what size the painting's canvas
needed to be. It turned out to be shy of life-size—actually thirty by forty
inches, though I couldn't have told you those exact dimensions at the time. I
knew I couldn't find a canvas that size in our little town, so I had to go to a
bigger town close by. And I went to several places in that town, as each one
referred me to yet another place where I might find what I was looking for,
which was quite a large canvas for any painter. Finally I found the right place,
and the salesperson asked, "Well, what size canvas do you want?"

I answered, "I don't know, but I will recognize it when I see it."

He kept bringing canvases of different sizes to me. And when he set down
the one that was the right size, I said, "That's it!"

And then he told me, "This one is thirty by forty."

Returning home with my canvas, I said to the Lord, "Lord, I don't know
how to paint anything like this, and I know that this is divine—from You.
So all I know to do is give You my heart and hands. And here are my paints.
Here's the canvas. I give it all to You. I surrender everything to You, and
this will be Your painting, not mine, because I don't have the ability to paint
something of this nature. But I know You want it painted, so here I am."

With a pencil in hand, I simply started sketching the vision the Lord had
given me in preparation for the oil painting that was to evolve. This work
of art actually sketched out easier than anything I had ever sketched before.
Then I began mixing paints and then applying the paints. In next to no time,
with no apparent effort at all, these three-dimensional, lifelike pots took
shape, with the hand above them seemingly reaching out of and beyond its

canvas confines to release water into the first of these. And just before the water entered that first pot, it turned into wine.

Within eight to ten hours, the assignment was completed. I stood back in awe to say, "God, what a magnificent painter You are," as I realized that I had just experienced the privilege of only holding the paintbrush as the Master Himself brought this painting to fruition. No credit was due me.

Later the Lord told me that this painting would be in many homes, which led me to believe that prints were to be made. But first I took this work of art to the local Bible bookstore managed by a friend of mine, and I asked him where I might be able to have prints made. I didn't know anything about having this done, but knew that God would provide what was needed for what He wanted done. It's just that most often we become His legs and arms and mouthpiece, and we have to be available and willing to ask, seek, and knock in order to receive, find, and have doors opened. (See Matthew 7:7.) Some people stay stuck and never see God accomplish what He wants done in, for, and through them because they are not willing to learn new things or to do things they've never done before. Leaving the original painting for a few hours with the Bible bookstore manager, I left to take care of business.

"OUTPOURING"

Standing with another man upon my return to the Bible bookstore, the manager exclaimed, "Oh, Valinda, I'm so glad you're here now. I was just telling this gentleman what your painting looked like."

I questioned, "You were *telling* him?"

"Yes," he replied.

Just then the other gentleman spoke up to explain, "I've lost my eyesight."

Expressing his belief that his loss of vision was only temporary and that God was going to restore it, this man went on to say that from what the store manager was telling him, my painting was quite a work of art. And then he told me that the most beautiful painting he ever saw was destroyed when the house that it was in burned. And then, quite surprisingly, this man asked, "Could you paint that painting for me?"

"Well, I don't know," I stated. "What did it look like?"

He described a globe on which God was pouring out His Spirit.

Thinking to myself that this was someone else's vision and that, unless God gave me that vision, I would not be able to paint it, I told this gentleman that I would have to pray about this. Taking my painting home, I had really put that gentleman's request aside, but that night I couldn't sleep. And the next night I couldn't sleep. And the next night I couldn't sleep. I kept thinking of that man. Walking the floor and walking the floor, I asked, "What is it, Lord?"

He informed me, "I want you to paint that painting. Go get the canvas."

I said, "Lord, You have to show me. I don't even know what the continents look like. I don't even know that I can draw a perfect circle, much less the continents."

"Go get the canvas!" I heard Him again say.

I purchased yet another thirty-by-forty-inch canvas and placed it in a little bitty place that I had set aside for doing my painting, and this time I told the Lord, "This is going to be more of a challenge than the other one."

© 2001 Yolinda Minick

"Outpouring"

I loved geography when I was in school, but it had been a *long* time since I had been in school. I had informed the Lord that I neither knew what the continents looked like nor where they were positioned—not exactly—and I didn't have anything in my house to go by. I didn't even have a compass for making a round circle.

187

"You and I are going to have to really wing this one," I told Him. "And, again, I give you my heart; I give you my hands and all of me. And here are the paints and the canvas."

I told the Lord that I didn't know where the continents were, but that He sure did—because He hung this world into space. "You know where they all are. So I trust You."

Before we sketched anything the Lord told me to paint the canvas black. I did know at that point that if you're painting water or a waterfall or something of that sort that you wanted to lighten up and make look fluid, you start with a black canvas. The Lord had said, "Paint it black," and then we started adding light.

By the time the painting was finished, even the locations of the mountain ranges were designated by thick, raised paint on the canvas's surface, and they were right where they were supposed to be. I later found some books to verify this. And once more I stood back in awe at what God had done.

I took this second painting to the Bible bookstore to show my friend, asking him to call the blind gentleman to tell him we had his painting ready. I couldn't help but think to myself, "Why would a blind man need a painting? But perhaps he could at least feel where the paint was textured and raised to represent the mountain ranges."

Leaving the painting at the bookstore, I ran my errands, only to return to a parking lot that was full. Entering the store, I was met by a lady ecstatically informing me, "Honey, you've got to come in this store. There's a painting in here, and there's a man in here that was blind and now can see. And he's seeing all kinds of things in this painting. I mean, we've had church in here."

And there in the midst was the man who had been blind, and he was seeing all kinds of things in this painting that I had not realized. He was saying, "Look! God didn't waste one thing of His Spirit; not one thing's wasted. Not one bit of His Spirit dropped off the earth."

He pointed out a dove with wings spread, perched on Jesus's arm. I hadn't, to my recollection, painted that dove there. I hadn't seen it until he pointed it out. He seemed to find all kinds of things in this painting—aptly titled "Outpouring"—that I didn't know were there.

"Redemption"

"REDEMPTION"

My third painting is most appropriately called "Redemption." Its inspiration came by way of a man who suffered an illness, the nature of which is not pertinent to this man's story in this book. This fellow was having a hard time believing God to heal him, because he actually believed his illness was a punishment handed down by God Himself.

On a certain occasion the Lord clearly said to me in regard to this gentleman, "Ask him if he's asked Me to heal him."

I didn't. I allowed myself to feel intimidated by this individual, for whom I had great respect and admiration. And then at a later time, the Lord said, "Ask him now!"

Once more I did not do what the Lord asked. And then, as my husband and I were parting ways with this fellow on yet another occasion, the Lord said again, "Ask him now!"

This time I merely patted this man on the back and said, "I'm going to be praying for you." As far as I was concerned, that in itself was a big, bold statement to be making to this particular person, as I actually expected him not to like one bit what I had just said but rather be insulted.

However, he responded by saying, "Good, 'cause you need the practice, and I need the prayer."

I felt about yea high. That was as much as I could get out. I wasn't about to ask, "Have you asked God to heal you?" But I knew I had disobeyed God—three times I disobeyed Him. I'll never do that again. For three days and three nights I did not sleep one wink—not *one* wink. I walked the floors day and night.

During this time my husband questioned, "What in the world are you doing? What is wrong with you?"

I explained to him that I had been up praying for this man, that I was supposed to have asked him on three different occasions if he had asked God to heal him. And then, knowing that my husband knew this man as well, I asked him if he would ask him this question for me.

"God didn't lay that on me," my husband said. "I'm not asking him. You ask him."

And all my further pleading with my husband got me nowhere in attempting to get him to take care of this for me. But God is so faithful. When we think He is mad at us or against us, He is chasing us down to show us how much He cares. An unusual twist of events resulted in me being on the telephone with this fellow giving him a message for someone else in regard to a change of schedule.

This fellow called, and I relayed the message, only to add, "Hold on a minute. I need to talk to you. Uh, I need to ask you something."

And he said, "You were supposed to ask me the other night, weren't you?"

"Yes. How'd you know?" I asked.

"I just know," was his reply. "Well, what did you want to ask me?"

And I said, "Well, you're probably going to think I'm some kind of religious nut, but I've just got to ask you. I haven't slept for three days and three nights because I didn't ask you. Have, uh, have you asked God to heal you?"

"Why would you ask me such a question as that?" he asked, like he was surprised.

I answered, "Because He told me to. He asked me to ask you."

"I just don't understand why you would ask me such a question as that," he continued.

Around and around we went, back and forth, until finally I put it bluntly:

"Well, *have you?*"

"No!"

"Well, why not?" I asked.

And this man proceeded to give me some "religious" explanation for why God had so inflicted him because he hadn't been faithful to Him like he should have—when, in all actuality, the man had not fallen into step with what "religion" thinks faithfulness looks like.

When I asked him if he *really* thought God had done this to him, his response was an emphatic, "Yeah!"

"That's a lie right out of the pits of hell!" I insisted, as I added that God did not do this to him. "What would He stand to gain from that? God *did not* do this to you. The devil did. Let me tell you something. God wants to heal you, and He will heal you *right now* if you ask Him.'"

It just jetted out of my mouth, "He will heal you *right now* if you will ask Him, 'cause He's not through with you yet."

And as soon as those words came out of my mouth, I looked to the Lord. "What are You saying, God? You had better be backing me up."

This man then said, "Well, I'm not going to go running to God now, because I haven't been doing what I was supposed to do. I'm not going to go whining and crying to God *now*."

I explained, "You don't understand. It's not really up to you. God's not through with you, and He wants to heal you. He's got plans for you."

And he said, "Well, I'm not going to whine to Him now."

"It isn't up to you," I repeated. "It's up to God. God wants to heal you. All you have to do is ask, and you will be healed."

"Well, I guess I have to ask, don't I?" he finally concurred.

"Yes, you do. You don't have a choice *if* you want to be healed."

And then he started to cry. Now, this conversation had been going on over the telephone for over an hour. And as soon as he started to cry, while holding that telephone receiver in my hand, I saw in a vision this regal, velvety, deep purple robe with a plush, jewel-encrusted border. It was just in front of my husband's recliner and suspended in midair. And I could tell by the folds in the robe that it was being held up by invisible hands. A ring, with a sizeable single jewel, was suspended in the air alongside the robe. It was all so reminiscent of the robe and ring that the father commanded his servants to place on the prodigal son upon his return home. (See Luke 15:22.)

I said to my friend on the other end of the phone, "Jesus is standing with a beautiful robe to wrap around you and a beautiful ring to place on your finger. All you have to do is to ask, and He will heal you and wrap this beautiful robe around you. All you have to do is ask."

Once he uttered his cry, "Oh, God, *heal me!*" right there on the spot God healed him. The next time I saw this man he picked me up and swung me around like I was a rag doll, drenching my shoulder with his tears.

The Lord I serve had not put this affliction on this man because of what this man thought was disobedience. Religion will talk us into walking right out from under God's love and grace, allowing some "religious" person or persons to talk us out of both of these and then enshroud us with guilt to the hilt. God's love and grace called for the robe and ring to be put on the prodigal son. Religion cripples and even kills our prodigal sons. Religion had set out to kill this amazingly wonderful man of God that I knew.

"OUR PURPOSE"

Until the writing of this book, there was a painting that I had never named—one of Jesus putting back together the broken pieces of clay pots. I had never had prints made of this painting like I did of my others. Until now, I felt like it was just for me. Perhaps I had to "get" its message before I could pass it on to others.

Broken pots lie scattered on the floor in this painting, with a few of their broken pieces lying on a table. As Jesus picks up one of the pots, it turns white in His hand, and He proceeds to cement its pieces back together with gold, the purest gold. That gold represents to me His blood, with all its healing and restoring power. In the background there's a pot, radiant and exquisite, as if on exhibit in a gallery—representative of how we will appear when we have become like Jesus and arrived in our new home to have glorified bodies, void of cracks filled with adhesives of any kind.

A certain Scripture comes to mind. In Romans 8:29 (KJV), we read, "For whom he did foreknow, he also did predestinate to be conformed to the image of his Son." The Amplified Bible speaks of being "molded into the image of His Son [and share inwardly His likeness]."

First John 3:2 (KJV) has something to add to this: "Beloved, now are we the sons of God, and it doth not yet appear what we shall be: but we know that when he shall appear, we shall be like him; for we shall see him as he is." This is what this painting is all about—our purpose here on Earth is to be conformed or molded to share the inward likeness of Jesus (both His nature and His character), that we might be shaped along the same lines that He is in order to, before it is all over, appear just like Him.

To become like Jesus is to have what is right, pure, lovely, beautiful, and full of peace for our individual lives. He *knows* all that we need. He *has* all that we need. So, if we have Him in our lives and allow Him to be in our lives *all* that He is—becoming inwardly like Him—then we have *all* we need. And what is in our heart will reflect outwardly. We will *appear* like Him. We will think like Him, talk like Him, walk like Him, act like Him. That is the highest, most noble aspiration one could have. And that's God's purpose for us here on the earth—nothing more, nothing less.

And that's what that painting of Jesus and the broken pots and the one pot in that gallery is all about—our purpose to be conformed to His likeness. That's my heart's cry, and very clearly and simply and in all its near-unbelievable, breathtaking beauty, this is the message that God wants me to share. Our purpose is to be like Jesus, whoever we are, whether carpenter or preacher or potter or evangelist. We may have different and other callings, but our ultimate goal is to be like Jesus, to be conformed to the image of God's Son. Thus, as I pen these words to this page, I now title this previously unnamed painting of Jesus and the broken pots and the one pot in the gallery "Our Purpose."

Chapter 48

TO BE LIKE JESUS

INDEED, JESUS IS the Way, the Truth, and the Life. (See John 14:6.) And to this very fact I ascribe all that has been true, honest, just, pure, lovely, and of good report in my earthly existence. I have come to know life—the abundant, full of peace and love and joy kind of life—that can only be derived from Him.

I walk in peace every day, all day, because I start my day spending time with my Lord. Sometimes He wakes me up at three or four o'clock in the morning to commune with Him. Sometimes He has big revelations to share. Sometimes He has visions to unfurl. But sometimes He and I, with my cup of coffee in hand, do not talk at all. He might not speak to me, and I might not speak to Him; rather, I just bask in the warmth of His presence. Nothing else is needed.

And three times a day, *at least* three times a day, I pray the Lord's Prayer. Jesus told His disciples in Matthew 6:9–13 (KJV) to pray after this manner:

> After this manner therefore pray ye: Our Father which art in heaven, Hallowed be thy name. Thy kingdom come, Thy will be done in earth, as it is in heaven. Give us this day our daily bread. And forgive us our debts, as we forgive our debtors. And lead us not into temptation, but deliver us from evil: For thine is the kingdom, and the power, and the glory, for ever. Amen.

For a long, long time, the Lord impressed upon me to not pray anything else. I tried to pray differently, and He'd ask me, "What's wrong with My prayer?"

And I would answer, "Nothing, Lord." I feel in my heart of hearts that He has had me praying His prayer because it is the most perfect prayer.

"Thy kingdom come, Thy will be done in earth, as it is in heaven." He wants His kingdom here on Earth—and now. And that's what He has kept trying to get me to understand, that His kingdom's not "way out there" like I used to think, that He's not some great big God way out there somewhere. I used to lay and look at the stars and think about a God who was way far away where those stars were. Little—no, not *at all*—did I realize that He was inside me as a born-again Christian and that He absolutely longed to walk with me and talk with me in the cool of the day, like He talked with Adam and Eve in the Garden.

An even more wonderful is the understanding that where God walked and talked *with* Adam and Eve in the Garden, He dwells *in* me and you. His Word says in 2 Corinthians 6:16 (KJV), "For ye are the temple of the living God; as God hath said, I will dwell *in* them, and walk *in* them; and I will be their God" (emphasis added). My ultimate purpose on Earth is to be conformed to the likeness of Jesus, who Himself said, "As thou, Father, art in me, and I in thee, that they also may be one in us" (John 17:21, KJV). That doesn't sound like a faraway God to me. The Father was in Jesus, and Jesus was in the Father—and so we were created for just that same kind of *close* relationship.

I just want people to understand the importance of having that personal one-on-one relationship with God, something that took me years to realize. I heard people say that they talked with God and that He told them this or that, and I thought, "Well, Lord, You don't talk to me. I don't know anything about all that stuff of 'God talked to me and told me this and that.'" I wondered if people were just making that up, because God didn't talk to me like that. I just didn't understand this. And until you have that kind of personal relationship with the Lord yourself you are likely to think that these people who say they talk to God and God talks to them have rocks in their head.

But the fact of the matter is that our Father longs for fellowship with us. He longs to express His love for us. And having been created by God, we, whether we realize it or not, long for Him as well. Only He, through Jesus, can fill that space in us that He and He alone is meant to fill. Unfortunately, many are trying to fill that space in their lives with something else.

If we would just steal away long enough each day to spend time with our Lord, even if it's no more than ten minutes, He's ever waiting to meet with us, whether we show up or not. Keeping an appointment with Him is to meet with the Prince of peace, the Giver of peace. With stress being a major cause of heart disease and other diseases galore, walking in the peace of God is a preventative and cure for sorrow, pain, and bad health.

Jesus is the Repairer and Restorer of broken pots—broken lives. He, through His precious blood, has made a way for us to return to relationship and fellowship with the Father, who has a robe and ring awaiting every prodigal son. Just as He wasted not one drop in pouring out His Spirit on the face of this earth, He wants to repair and build back like new the waste places in our lives. His Word even tells us that "instead of their shame my people will receive a double portion…they will inherit a double portion in their land" (Isa. 61:7). The Amplified Bible says, "Instead of your [former] shame you shall have a twofold recompense…in their land they shall possess double [what they had forfeited]." He wants to turn our water into wine, to give us not that which is merely leftover, only salvageable, even our just desserts—but to give us the best *last*, even *now*.

When my boys were young and small, I didn't have much money. Jigsaw puzzles were affordable, so I bought a lot of them. And Phil and Spence just loved to stick a piece of the puzzle under their leg so they could be the one to put the last piece of the puzzle in place.

I have found God to be a lot like my boys in that respect, except He is not hiding from us what we need. He is our Creator, and only He has the piece or pieces that will make us complete. If we will allow, He is eager and willing and ever-ready to surprise us with the piece of the puzzle that appears missing and is needed to make some picture complete in our lives. But not only that, He knows what the cover of the puzzle box looks like. He knows all, from beginning to end. He knows what the final picture should look like. He knows what we need most. He knows what we need that will be best; not just good or better, but best.

It is my prayer that my story will be a puzzle piece—maybe several puzzle pieces—in the hand of God for the fulfilling of *your* story. You have one, you know, and not that it will necessarily be delivered by way of a book or a craft such as pottery-making. Instead of a pot, yours may be a symphony or a poem. It may be delivered from a lectern or from behind an office desk or on a sports field or with a paintbrush and canvas. It may be delivered with cookware and recipes or a mop and broom. It may be delivered with a hammer and nail or a needle and thread. It may be delivered through a combination of all sorts of abilities and opportunities and venues.

But you do have a story, one that was purposed in the heart of God to be found in your knowing His Son and being conformed to His nature and character. One that cannot find fulfillment apart from Him, apart from "being rooted and established in [His] love" (Eph. 3:17). One where you have a place in the heart of God that no one else can fill. One that He and He alone can make complete. He has the cover to your box, and He has the puzzle pieces you need.

I challenge you to "own" your story, to "own" your place in God's heart—a place that is found only through His Son, Jesus. It is there that your wildest dreams and imaginations and ultimate fulfillment will be found. It is there that you will find all the purpose, peace, power, and provision that you will ever need, no matter how great the miracle required. *I know.* You've read my story: I am a miracle! And you can have one, even *be* one, too!

As a matter of fact, my being a miracle makes my story a miracle story. Therefore, as long as this book is in your possession, you will *always* have a miracle!

NOTES

Introduction

1. Michelle Coakes, *Creative Pottery* (Gloucester: Rockport Publishers, Inc., 1998), Preface.

Chapter 2: Abuse and Dysfunctional Theology

1. Michael Yaconelli, *Messy Spirituality* (Grand Rapids: Zondervan, 2002), 69.

2. Maxine O'Dell Gernert, "Pentecost Confronts Abuse," *Journal of Pentecostal Theology*, Issue 17 (2000): 120.

3. Walter Brueggemann, *Finally Comes the Poet: Daring Speech for Proclamation* (Minneapolis: Fortress Press, 1989), 24.

4. Gernert, 121.

5. Ibid., 130.

6. Ibid., 123.

7. Ibid., 122.

Chapter 4: The Banty Hen and Her Chicks

1. Anne Lamott, *Traveling Mercies: Some Thoughts on Faith* (New York: Pantheon, 1999), 49–50.

2. Ibid.

Chapter 5: Created for Love

1. Yaconelli, 13.

2. Dr. LaDonna Osborn (Osborn Ministries International Headquarters, Tulsa, OK), interview by Bobbie Jo Hamilton, December 19, 2009.

3. *Webster's New Universal Unabridged Dictionary* (New York: Barnes & Noble Books, 2003), 1277.

4. Wayne Jacobsen, *He Loves Me* (Newbury Park: Windblown Media, 2007), 114.

Chapter 7: Understanding Suicide

1. "Suicide," *Wikipedia, the free encyclopedia*, available at http://en.wikipedia. org/wiki/Suicide (accessed March 17, 2012).

Chapter 15: Getting Rid of the Victim Mentality

1. "Quotes by Frank Outlaw," http://strangewondrous.net/browse/author/o/outlaw+frank

2. "Mr. Holland's Opus," *Wikipedia, the free encyclopedia*, available at http://en.wikipedia.org/wiki/Mr._Holland's_Opus (accessed March 17, 2012).

Chapter 16: Closed Head Injury

1. "Closed Head Injury, *Wikipedia, the free encyclopedia*, available at http://en.wikipedia.org/wiki/ Closed_head_ injury (accessed March 17, 2012).
2. Ibid.
3. Ibid.

Chapter 18: Strong Connection Between Pottery and People

1. Coakes, 34.
2. John Dickerson, *Pottery Making, a Complete Guide* (New York: The Viking Press, 1974), 13.
3. Ibid.
4. Coakes, 14.
5. Ibid., 33.
6. Dickerson, 10–11,13–14.
7. Ibid., 10–11.
8. Ibid., 9.
9. Ibid., Introduction.

Chapter 24: A Negligent Doctor and the Flesh-Eating Disease

1. "Peritonitis," *Wikipedia, the free encyclopedia*, available at http://en.wikipedia.org/wiki/Peritonitis (accessed March 17, 2012).
2. Ibid.
3. Paul A. Johnson, "Flesh-Eating Disease Health Article," *Yahoo! Health*, http://health.yahoo.net/galecontent/flesh-eating-disease (accessed March 17, 2012).
4. Ibid.
5. "Necrotizing Fasciitis," *Wikipedia, the free encyclopedia*, available at http://en.wikipedia.org/wiki/Necrotizing_fasciitis (accessed May 9, 2012).
6. Ibid.
7. Majeski J., "Necrotizing Fasciitis Developing from a Brown Recluse Spider Bite," US National Library of Medicine National Institutes of Health, http://www.ncbi.nlm.nih.gov/pubmed/11243548.
8. "Necrotizing Fasciitis," *Wikipedia*.

Chapter 30: Swimming With the Dolphins

1. "Flatline," *Wikipedia, the free encyclopedia*, available at http://en.wikipedia.org/wiki/Flatline (accessed March 17, 2012).
2. "Sleep apnea," *Wikipedia, the free encyclopedia*, available at http://en.wikipedia.org/wiki/Sleep_apnea (accessed March 17, 2012).

CHAPTER 32: FORGING A WAY

1. "Arteriogram," *Medline Plus, Trusted Health Information for You,* http://www.nlm.nih.gov/medlineplus/ency/article/003327.htm (accessed May 9, 2012).
2. "Echocardiography," *Wikipedia, the free encyclopedia,* available at http://en.wikipedia.org/wiki/Echocardiography (accessed March 17, 2012).
3. Jacobsen, 3.

CHAPTER 33: WAITING FOR THE SON

1. Yaconelli, 96.
2. Ibid., 98.
3. Col Stringer, *On Eagles* [sic] *Wings* (Jacksonville: Col Stringer Ministries, 1997), 68.

CHAPTER 41: IT'S A MESSAGE OF GRACE

1. Jacobsen, 137.

CHAPTER 46: LETTING GO

1. "Noah Was a Drunk and Isaac Was a Daydreamer," http://bohemianalien.wordpress.com/2007/11/09/noah-was-a-drunk-and-isaac-was-a-daydreamer.

ABOUT THE AUTHOR

VALINDA MIRACLE IS a wife, mother, grandmother, marketplace success as an accomplished ceramics artisan, and a true woman of God with a BIG heart for evangelism. Her Miracle Pottery and Art Gallery is tucked on a hillside in the foothills of Mentone in Valley Head, Alabama. As already stated, a number of traumatic and near-death experiences, including a tremendous handicap, positioned this woman for anything but the success story that is hers today. She may have "bled," but the enemy didn't win.

CONTACT THE AUTHOR

miraclepottery.com